The *Easy Way* to Learn Astrology

T0024802

"Concentrating solely on Signs and Houses makes total sense, and it's fun, too. Alison's casual and entertaining style of writing takes the reader by the hand and allays any fears of a supposedly complex subject. What you get is in-depth knowledge of the twelve zodiac signs, including polarities, elements, and qualities, plus the workings and meanings of the two main axes, quadrants, and twelve houses in the chart. As an introduction to astrology, this is a great book."

—KARIN HOFFMANN, editor for
Astrodienst on **www.astro.com**

"Alison taught me astrology using this system and it immediately clicked. Now I am a paid astrological influencer on YouTube. I highly recommend it to reach professional status."

—PENNY DIX, astrologer and psychotherapist

The *Easy Way* to Learn ASTROLOGY

How to Read Your Birth Chart

ALISON CHESTER-LAMBERT, M.A.

 FINDHORN PRESS

Findhorn Press
One Park Street
Rochester, Vermont 05767
www.findhornpress.com

Text stock is SFI certified

Findhorn Press is a division of Inner Traditions International

---

Disclaimer

The information in this book is given in good faith and intended for information only. Neither author nor publisher can be held liable by any person for any loss or damage whatsoever which may arise directly or indirectly from the use of this book or any of the information therein.

Cataloging-in-Publication data for this title is available from the Library of Congress

ISBN 979-8-88850-039-2 (print)
ISBN 979-8-88850-040-8 (ebook)

Printed and bound in the United States by Lake Book Manufacturing, LLC
The text stock is SFI certified. The Sustainable Forestry Initiative® program promotes sustainable forest management.

10 9 8 7 6 5 4 3 2 1

Edited by Jacqui Lewis
Illustrations, text design and layout by Richard Crookes
This book was typeset in Adobe Garamond Pro, Helvetica Neue, and Avenir Book

To send correspondence to the author of this book, mail a first-class letter to the author c/o Inner Traditions • Bear & Company, One Park Street, Rochester, VT 05767, USA and we will forward the communication, or contact the author directly at **www.alisonchesterlambert.com**.

Contents

"If I have seen further,
it is by standing on the shoulders of giants."
– Isaac Newton, 1675

I thank all my early teachers for their devotion to astrology and their legacy.

During my student years, around the millennium, I read so many astrology books and attended so many lectures and schools. I would learn them all by heart, and they have all contributed to my current knowledge. I do hope that I have not inadvertently used their words exactly or not cited them properly.

A special thank you goes to the team at **astro.com** for re-engineering their website to allow the special features that this planet-free, *Campanus* system needs for it to work in the early days of learning astrology.

Preface

Ever *Tried* to Learn Astrology?

That's because the usual teaching methods have not moved out of the last century. There is an easier, more intuitive way to present it, but the old teachers think that struggle is par for the course. I am dyslexic and a very slow learner. I tried and failed to learn astrology twice when I was younger. After I turned 40 and felt more confident, I enrolled on a classroom course. That got me going, and, finally, sheer determination slowly opened that incredible door.

When my opportunity came to teach, I knew that I had to do it differently. To learn psychological astrology, we have to dive deeply into the origins and structures underlying the behaviour of the cosmos. This enables us to achieve happier outcomes by understanding and modifying our behaviour.

Why make students learn the mathematical process of drawing a birth chart by hand, when computers now do that job for us? Fortunately, the "old-school" astrologers rejected me, so I was forced to do my own thing.

After successfully teaching dozens of students, I recognized that most people want to learn because they have already dabbled in Sun signs, so why not learn the zodiac signs first? Something easy to recognize and non-threatening. Why make it hard, when it can be easy?

All you will need to learn astrology is this book. Then find the **astro.com** website; this will give you access to the software that can construct a chart for you, online, for free.

There is a Facebook product page for this book, where I will be able to answer any questions you may have; search for "The EASY WAY to Learn Astrology." I also offer a string of free videos to go with this package. You can find me under my name on YouTube.

It is important to note before we go any further that there are many astrologies, including medieval astrology, Vedic astrology, and the monthly Sun sign predictions in magazines. Each has its differences and merits and every single one has value. This book, however, teaches psychological astrology.

So let's go . . .

A Note on Astrological Terms

Throughout this book, the Sun and Moon have initial capital letters, as do Masculine and Feminine to differentiate them as the names of the two polarities, and the Elements to avoid confusion with terrestrial fire, water, earth, and air.

It is important to note that throughout this book I am not referring to Sun signs; the descriptions and discussions are of the zodiac signs themselves, all of which we have in our birth charts. For example, you can be what I call a "Taurean type" even if you were born in February and have your Sun in Aquarius.

It All Starts with Oneness

Ancient Hindu mysteries tell us the singularity, the source, the perfect one-ness, is a blissful state of deity that was there in the beginning. Astrophysics is a little less poetic, declaring that the primordial soup exploded with a Big Bang and formed our dimension.

However, it doesn't matter if you are a scientist or the Dalai Lama, the language of astrology copes easily with all belief systems. Whether it be a blissful union with deity, or a chemically fecund gas in space, astrology simply accepts an undifferentiated state of "one."

I believe cosmos is formless thought. An all-pervading, mutifaceted manifestation from which energies, emanations, or essences emerge.

Everything in this dimension, space, and universe (Uni-verse) exists in the oneness. So that's Heaven, Hell, the Duat of the Egyptians, Greek Olympus . . . And, importantly, the dark energy and dark matter of quantum physics. Important because that is how astrology works.

The Division into Two, Polarity or Duality

A duality means made up of two parts. Science recognizes that we live in a duality. In quantum mechanics, a duality of wave and particle are recognized; it acknowledges an emitter and a receiver. Electrical current has a positive and negative characteristic, seen in the two separate ends of a battery. And of course, we have the Taoist symbol of yin and yang, while the two sexes seen in nature seem fairly clear-cut.

As you can see in Figure 1, astrology recognizes the division of one into two opposites—Masculine and Feminine. It is true to say that in understanding "the opposite," we can gain a good comprehension of both sides. What is, versus what is not. I am this, I am *not* that.

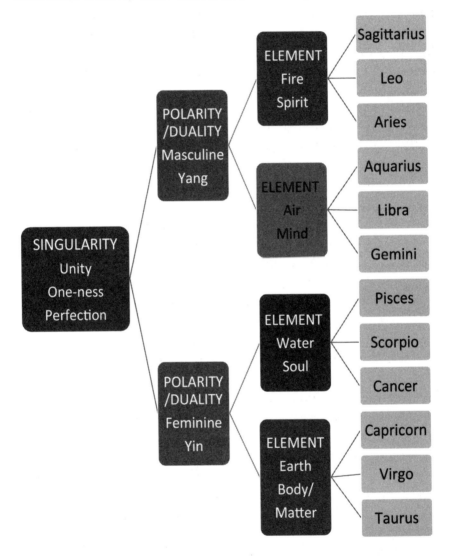

Fig. 1: The Spiritual and Astrological Hierarchy Table

The Psychology of Masculine and Feminine Behaviour

Understand the psychology of Masculine and Feminine and you are halfway to understanding a birth chart. For it all boils down to how much Masculine and how much Feminine a person was born with and how they use it. It is that simple. And years from now, when you are captivated by some rare, technical, sexy, astrological chart point and you are wailing with frustration, remember these words. Go back to basics and look at the weighting and combination of Masculine and Feminine energies. It is all there.

The term Masculine in astrology is describing a type of energy and it doesn't rely on a person's sex. There are females with overwhelming amounts of Masculine energy and males with oceans of Feminine energy. Your job is to figure out how that works for them. And it really doesn't matter whether or not a person identifies with their birth sex. You can still help them understand themselves better by understanding the combination of Masculine and Feminine energies in the multilayered language of astrology.

Yes, there is a general truth that women will express their Feminine more easily than men do, while men will "hide" theirs. And women who were born with lots of Masculine may struggle to find a welcoming place in the world for it, while men born with lots of Masculine are deemed to be commanding and decisive and will be promoted to the board of directors within months. It has been like that for all of my life, but the boundaries are blurring now and hopefully the future will be different.

There is nothing in a birth chart that will reveal whether a person is a biological male or a biological female. What we have to understand is what they were born to express and work with in their particular mix of Feminine and Masculine energy, and then how this fits with their sex generally.

In Figure 2, we can see key words for Masculine and Feminine. Considering the ones next to each other in one row, it becomes obvious that they describe two sides of the same coin. Masculine is extroverted and Feminine is introverted, etc. It is worth keeping a photo of that

Masculine +	Feminine −
Yang	Yin
Positive	Negative
Maleness	Femaleness
Sky/height/ upwards/outwards	Valley/depth/ downwards/inwards
Moves in straight lines	Moves in curves, spirals
Light	Dark
Conscious	Unconscious
Seeks freedom	Seeks boundaries
Extroverted	Introverted
Surges outwards—radiation	Pulls in—gravity
Rebuffs	Receptive
Active	Passive
Separates	Joins together
Pushes away	Holds in
Initiates	Waits
Spontaneous	Long-term planning
Direct	Indirect
Open	Conceals
Assertive	Timid
Confident	Unsure
Believes in self	Doubts self
The FIRE and AIR ELEMENTS are Masculine	The WATER and EARTH ELEMENTS are Feminine

Fig. 2: Polarity or Duality

list on your phone so you can keep referring to it. Get used to thinking about daily life in those terms.

Possibly the most useful way to imagine Masculine is solar radiation pouring outwards from the Sun. And gravity is Feminine in nature, always pulling everything into the centre.

Too much Masculine is destructive, and too much Feminine is equally destructive. Neither is "better" than the other. That would be like saying one end of a battery is better than the other end.

The Hero's Journey in mythology is a tale of Masculinity, while the female tending the home in his absence is indeed Femininity. Neither role is easy.

Figure 3 examines the result of too much Feminine or too much Masculine and is worth a little thought.

Extreme Feminine	Extreme Masculine
Overwhelming feelings	Lack of feelings
Seething emotion	Emotionally cut off
Uncontrollable, consuming desire	The cold act of extreme violence
Clawing for response	Psychopathy
Devouring, wrathful, ugly	Utopian vision of extreme perfection
Need to possess	Self-centred indifference
Destructive	Destroying

Fig. 3: Keywords for Extreme Feminine and Masculine

Now let us consider how Masculine and Feminine come together in myth. Well, it depends which is doing the chasing! When Feminine wants the liaison for procreative purposes (the Feminine oversees death and birth), it cannot simply grab for it as Masculine would. Feminine works in curves, not straight lines. If a person is employing their Feminine energy, they will use sexual guile and quiet allure. If a person is using their Masculine energy they will move directly into the chase. A little coaxing might be in order, but their actions will be overt.

Now remember, females can be Masculine in behaviour and males can be Feminine. Masculine with a capital M is describing an energy and behaviour, not males in general. Feminine with a capital F is also describing an energy and a behaviour, not females in general.

Let's look at another example. How about a general in the army planning a military campaign? Sounds Masculine, right? Maybe, if it is short-term planning. But . . . long-term planning is a Feminine function because of the hidden agenda, the patience and waiting required. The Masculine can't wait for that sort of thing, it just picks up a weapon and strikes. His Masculine side will be doing the short-term, punchy bits, and his Feminine will be giving him the guile for the unrevealed long-term plan.

Now let's examine the Feminine cycle of life. Something very particular to the Feminine. This has a primordial feel to it. I am reminded of an ancient wisdom, found in Ancient Egyptian and Greek religious material, that the dark of the Feminine exists before all. It is origin, it is the primal material. In the beginning of our universe the light of Masculine *happens* to the Feminine. The active force stirs the dark, primordial water. I'm taking nothing away from the Masculine here, because the Feminine was going nowhere without the action of the Masculine. In the Old Testament, the light/intention of the Masculine hovered over the waters of the Feminine and that stirred things up. Feminine's inertia needed some action, or we would all still be cosmic "mud."

So . . . Let's just accept that the Feminine, or Mother Nature, has a "plan" or a preprogrammed agenda and that Masculine actually doesn't. To Masculine, spontaneity is everything. The capricious will of the gods prevails. Not so with Mother Nature.

A quick browser search will reveal that roughly 68 per cent of the universe is dark energy. Dark matter makes up about 27 per cent. The rest—everything on Earth, everything ever observed with all of our instruments, all normal matter—adds up to less than 5 per cent of the universe. So all we know is the tip of the iceberg. And by the way, dark energy is the equivalent of the Fire Element and dark matter is the equivalent of the Water Element in this astrology.

Dark energy and dark matter are in another dimension, which underpins our universe. All mythological "dark" places are referring to this. So, Christian Hell, Norse Hel, the Egyptian Duat, Greek Tartarus, Hades, etc., are in this other side to life. In astrology, the planet Pluto rules dark energy and matter, and the zodiac sign of Scorpio is associated with the same.

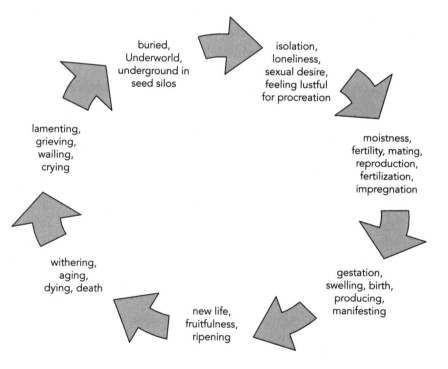

Fig. 4: The Cycle of the Feminine, Life, and Mother Nature

The Cycle of Life and the Feminine that we see in Figure 4 is a slow, persistent, continually evolving process. An all-pervading force in the Universe that receives, gestates, and gives birth to life.

At various stages, the primordial Feminine invokes howling rage, wrath, vengeance, brutality, primordial instinct, outrage, or desperation. But it also invokes love, caring, emotion, sharing, compassion, and support. As Queen Elizabeth II said, grief is the price we pay for love. This is all in the Feminine continuum.

It is primordial, and it is rich with creative potential because, most of all, the Feminine **creates**, it is a creatrix. It keeps moving and evolving. The bud of next year's twig is behind the falling leaf. As we lose one thing, another appears. Nature fills empty spaces.

Evolution is a slow, unseen Feminine process; it happens gradually and continually over a long period of time.

Revolution, on the other hand, implies sudden, unexpected changes involving action, a radical turnaround, or some kind of break-up for the status quo. And there we see Masculine energy.

Astrology has a Feminine planet representing evolution and a Masculine planet that represents revolution.

The Zodiac Signs of the Zodiac Belt

When the astrology we know today was developed, in the latter half of the first millennium BCE, a ring around the Earth, called the zodiac belt, was established. It is a framework built upon the effect that the Sun's rays have on the Earth during the course of a year.

As any old Druid around Stonehenge or the Celtic Isles will tell you, the winter solstice, the spring equinox, the summer solstice, and the autumnal equinox mark out the four days during the year that the Sun will reach an important point. These four points are the cardinal directions of north, south, east, and west and they form a cross around us in the sky.

The early astrologers took that cross and divided each of the four quarters (quadrants) into three smaller sections. So, the circle of the zodiac belt was divided into 12 equal portions around Earth. And that's it. It really is that simple. We see the Sun and planets *through* those 12 zodiac signs.

Another way to put it: the zodiac signs of Aries, Taurus, Gemini, Cancer, Leo, Virgo, Libra, Scorpio, Sagittarius, Capricorn, Aquarius, and Pisces are simply 12 portions of the sky around the Earth. In the practice of astrology, each is a **psychological force or energy**. Think of them as having different colours. So, using the Sun as an example, the rays of the Sun shine through the colour or energy of the zodiac sign.

Unfortunately, the names for the zodiac signs were copied from the constellations or patterns of stars further out in the sky. That has led to terrible confusion ever since, because astronomers, for instance, think that Aries is a constellation or pattern of stars in the sky. To astrologers it is a portion of the sky around Earth and *nothing at all* to do with the constellation or pattern of stars. This unfortunate duplication of names occurs for all the zodiac signs.

The Difference between Sun Signs and Zodiac Signs

So, the word "Signs" always means the zodiac signs. These days we don't use the full term very much; we use its shortened form.

So, what does "Sun sign" mean? Before I answer that, I must explain that we have more than one astrology. We have very many astrologies. Plural. Lots of them.

You have probably heard the term Sun sign astrology in weekly or monthly horoscope columns in newspapers or magazines. This kind of astrology uses the sign (the part of the sky) the Sun was in at the person's birth, and constructs different but readable charts from that. We have to thank the Sun sign astrologers for keeping astrology alive in the mainstream since the early twentieth century, whether or not it was a little bit vague. But critics of astrology usually ask how one-twelfth of the population could all have the same prediction.

The Birth Chart or Horoscope

This is a map of the planets, space objects, and zodiac signs at the moment of a person's birth. It also includes another division of the 360 degrees of a circle around the person into 12 uneven segments called houses. To read this map, we have to know the psychological meaning of each of the signs and houses. This is enough for now; we can add the planets and space objects later. There are other astrological interpretations too, but this is about psychological astrology so we will just stick to that.

Just in case you are tempted to go straight to the signs you know and ignore the rest, let me explain that we all have every sign in our birth charts, so you really will have to know them all by heart.

The Four Elements of Fire, Earth, Air, and Water

If you have a quick look at Figure 1, you will see that the two polarities of Masculine and Feminine divide into four Elements, two being Masculine and two being Feminine.

The two Masculine Elements are Fire and Air. The two Feminine Elements are Water and Earth. So oneness has now become four.

The two most spiritual Elements are Masculine Fire and Feminine Water and we can identify their presence both in our dimension, and also in the invisible or "dark" quantum realms that underpin ours.

Everything that comes after this, all the zodiac signs, houses and planets are all ruled by one of these four Elements. And given that they are mainly all Masculine or Feminine, you already know a lot about them. For instance, Fire and Air are active and surge outwards, they are direct and open. Water and Earth, however, hold things in, they are cautious and patient.

The Elements describe the motivation behind a person's actions and choices. Here are a few keywords for each element worth remembering:

Fire	Air	Earth	Water
Attention	Detachment	Practicality	Attachment
Enthusiasm	Scrutiny	Realism	Sensitivity
Confidence	Logic	Reliability	Compassion
Drama	Friendliness	Calm	Secrecy
Warmth	Sociability	Restraint	Emotion

Fig. 5: Keywords for the Four Elements

The Element of Fire

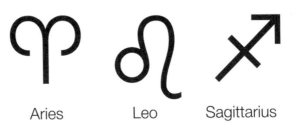

Aries   Leo   Sagittarius

Fig. 6: The Fire Signs

For the purposes of this book, can we accept that spirit is Fire and pure energy? All deity resides here, and belief and attention are the most crucial factors. When we give Fire attention, we are working with it. The power of belief probably needs no introduction here!

Let's think about the Fire we see in this dimension. Show a baby fire and it is mesmerized. Fire is colourful and dramatic and lights up the dark. Because it is so volatile and unpredictable, it cannot easily be contained, a reminder that it is an outgoing Masculine energy. Always hot and untouchable, it captivates attention and stirs the senses. We should remember that the fire in the grate doesn't stop to ask, "Which bit of coal shall I burn next?," it just burns whatever it touches without hesitation. This is the essence of the self-centredness of the Fire Element. It defers to no one.

Fire signs have energy, life force, and spirit. All three are very quick and hate waiting. They don't spend time thinking or weighing things up, they just move forward confidently and instinctively. This is about intuition or "gut" reactions rather than thinking, and this is the way Fire "thinks:" it intuits.

Mind, language, and conscious analysis come under the Element of Air and are a separate function to the special gut intuition of Fire, which is faster and uncanny. Thanks to recent research, we now know that the gut is the second brain of the body. It is lined with a network of neurons that are part of the enteric nervous system. Hence, discussion about gut intuition and reactions is no longer scoffed at by scientists.

If you have ever been shopping with a fiery person, you may have noticed how they buy an item of clothing. Instead of pausing and holding it up in front of a mirror, they just grab it as they are passing and head for the checkout. No trying it on or matching it up with accessories. They seem to know what they want in nanoseconds, which is just as well because they don't like taking anything back to the shop. Returning anything is going over old ground and Fire hates to look backwards or admit it made the wrong decision.

It is worth looking again at the sentence: *The fire in the grate doesn't stop to ask, "Which piece of coal shall I burn next?"* It is the speed of fire that helps us understand the psychology of this Element. Fire likes opportunities for action and exploration, challenges, things to burn up, and doors to go through. Their contagious enthusiasm attracts admirers.

The forward-looking nature of Fire is blessed with a creative vision that does not necessarily pander to realistic potential. Realism is left to the Earth Element, for practicality is not a feature of Fire's realm. This is where dreams are made, with all the visionary potential of *Sleeping Beauty* and the hopefulness of a child before Christmas.

Fire knows that anything and everything is possible; it can be, it can move into and out of existence, and the possibilities arising out of this are limitless. In this world of dreams and potential, the gods actually *do* reward believers with a degree of some success. And so we approach the subject of *belief*, and how that belief can spin reality. There is a line in a song that states that "Once conceived, once believed, fantasy is reality's childhood, and like a seed, visions need constant care . . . "

There is no doubt that our beliefs assist in forming the future. Experiments by quantum physicists confirm that the attention given by the observer brings a potential into "reality."

Belief in deity and homage to those gods increases the bounty that befalls us. Praise and gratitude actually nourish the existence of divinity. Greek manuscripts from around the seventh century BCE write of the need to keep humans alive and worshipping the god/desses so that the Olympus pantheon survives. In a world of "you scratch my back and I'll scratch yours," the Fire signs have an innate belief that they can take risks because their god/desses will save them. Is that what we call luck? Yup, I think so.

And while we are on the subject, we might as well address the inherent belief that the Fire Element and its three zodiac signs "know" that they are god/dess-like, if not directly related to the Supreme Being. This is a simple fact for those humans who are born to act out the Fire Element and they can't see a problem with it. They are the absolute centre of their lives, and so they are "self"-centred. Don't forget, there is divine energy in this Element. Fire is spirit, the spirit that hovers over the Water Element in the Book of Genesis.

As a result, those who get to live a life using or expressing the Fire Element as a part of themselves have great faith in themselves, unending strength of purpose, and a very direct honesty. These guys are not manipulative; they can usually get what they want by going straight for it, so they don't need subterfuge to win.

Imagine a meeting with a plate of biscuits in the centre of the table. The biscuits are dry and boring except for two chocolate biscuits right on the top. While Earth and Water are secretly working on deceptive tactics to get the chocolate ones without appearing obvious, Fire simply leans over and takes both the biscuits, saying "Oh, I love chocolate, I'll save the other one for later!"

There are, of course, some drawbacks to having a Fire powerhouse within. Fiery people cannot stare at detail for too long without pushing back their chair and bursting out of confinement. Their boredom threshold is very low and this makes them unreliable and lacking in self-control.

At that point, you may get trampled on or scorched if you are in the way. It's not that Fire is insensitive—it is often horrified that it has hurt you—but it must reach for freedom from the banal, drab, detailed, and boring. The all-encompassing need to burn brightly means that it sometimes just can't think about anyone else. This feels like insensitivity if you are on the receiving end. Fiery people can come across as wilful and overpowering. They can rush into things with such haste that they unintentionally cause destruction or hurt feelings.

Limited thinking, discipline, and rigidity will also cause Fire to rebel. Fire affirms itself, "I am right, what I know is right, what I want is right!" In their opinion, rules are meant to be broken. Fire is impatient with, and scornful of, authority. Anyone in a superior position is automatically dismissed with scathing comments. Fire likes to think it is the most superior being in the world.

Another drawback to being the brightest button in the box is the tendency to exaggerate and overdramatize everything. Everything they say can be halved or doubled, because Fire *likes* things brightly and attractively coloured, and needs to animate this drab old world with fantasy and funny stories. It is just too boring otherwise. Others soon get to realize that Fiery people cannot be trusted to tell the truth, and this gets embarrassing for the Fire person who would like to be admired alongside Zeus but could reasonably be called a liar.

However, Fire will carry on embellishing the stories, even if there is no one left to listen. The dreams and fantasies are as necessary to Fire as the sea is to a fish. Just as surely as the fish would die without water, Fire is snuffed out and extinguished without *belief* in dreams, visions, and fantasy. And that is not just a sad thing to behold, it is crisis territory for Fire and spirit. Our world is built on *belief* and *attention*. Don't forget, our belief in Fire/spirit and the attention we give to the divinities within it keep it going. It is like inflating a balloon, instead of watching it crumple into a sliver of thin rubber.

Having covered belief, let's look at attention-needs now. Those blessed with a good amount of Fire in their birth charts need a special kind of attention, or they will have confidence issues and the Fire within will struggle to express itself, leaving them a lost shadow of what they could be in life.

This attention, call it "red love," needs to be found in the adoring eyes and voice of a Fire child's parents throughout babyhood and childhood. This is particularly important if the child has a big helping of the Fire zodiac sign Leo in their birth chart. The child needs praise simply for being special, rather than achieving, and loads of it. We will cover this in greater detail in the Leo section.

Suffice it to say for now that the Fire/spirit within every one of us should be revered, nourished, and treasured. If you realize this was probably missing in your childhood, it is not too late to give your inner child "red love" by acknowledging your specialness, your importance, and your amazing spirit.

A last word now on Fire's relationship with the material world, which is shaky at best. Because of the incorporeal, spiritual, energy-based nature of Fire, it has no experience of being encased in a material body. So, Fire is not comfortable in skin and doesn't have a good relationship with bodies, which are a nuisance and an irritating mystery. I got this very revealing comment from someone who is nearly all Fire energy and remembers thinking this about their body at a very young age. "What is this cold, wet place I have been put in? So heavy and miserable. So demanding and restrictive."

"Gosh!" said I.

So, we can take from this that Fire has no idea how to cope with a body. Fire doesn't want to keep it in one piece either. Someone with a lot of Fire in their birth chart happily goes for surgical removal of anything that irritates them. Since Fire is impatient with bodily limitations and old age, these are also the guys to fill the waiting rooms of plastic surgeons with a quest to look forever young. Or they can want to subject their body to myriad tattoos and piercings while still young, perhaps trying to express their Fire instincts of uniqueness, or trying to assert their control over a body they are unhappy with. Whatever the reason, sometimes they choose not to leave the body alone; they have issues with it.

So, what happens when the body gets sick? All Fiery people are hopeless with illness, their own or anyone else's. How dare that body do something it shouldn't! Zeus should not have to deal with this. Hence, they generally leave it to someone more earthy to clean up and do the healing of the body. If Fire people do anything at all, it is usually the wrong thing!

Fire's pain centres on lack of social position, lack of importance, lack of accolade.

~ ARIES ~
Fire Zodiac Sign

Glyph ♈
First Sign of the Zodiac Belt
First Fire Sign
"I am"
Ruled by Mars
Symbol is the Ram

This chapter does not refer to Aries as a Sun sign but to the Aries energy that exists in all of us to a degree. Ariens or the Aries types discussed here simply have more of it than most.

The Aries energy is fast, spontaneous, energetic, pioneering, and very centred to self. Aries-type people will put themselves first when they want something. What Aries wants, Aries gets. It is impulsive, with an urgent need for self-assertion and autonomy. A simple, uncomplicated, black-and-white, all-or-nothing energy.

All zodiac signs are ruled by a planet, and Aries is ruled by Mars the god of war, so we shouldn't be surprised that Aries loves a battle and will fight enthusiastically for a cause. Brandishing a sword, Aries will leap headlong into the fray. This battle could be for a worthy cause (or a selfish cause!) such as deprived children, the sick and downtrodden in life, or maybe just the underdog.

But it is society's governance that really gets their goat . . . or ram. Laws, tax collecting systems, health systems, central government, local government, or any community decision-making vehicle for that matter, will become a target for Aries's withering and contemptuous comments.

Aries energy moves so quickly, it is astonishing. Simple things like having a shower or hanging washed clothes out to dry are achieved in record time. I once watched an Arien friend put a tent up in minutes without the instructions, while the rest of us were still getting the bits out of the cars.

It is a simple, pure, Masculine-oriented energy. Imagine a caveman going out, clubbing the beast and dragging it back to the lair. And if the beast puts up a good fight and Aries still wins, all the better. Having said that, Ariens wouldn't like to be thought of as crude and brutish, more crusading and gallant.

We will never have the birth chart of Robin Hood, who robbed from the rich and gave to the poor in the thirteenth century, but it would likely have a good helping of Aries energy in it. A chart we do have is that of Emma Watson, who starred as Hermione Granger in the Harry Potter films; she has a chunk of exaggerated Aries in her birth chart and has become a global female activist.

Keira Knightley is another good example because, although some of her acting roles have been pretty sedate, the heavy emphasis on her Aries energy can be seen in a staggering list of credits for activism including Amnesty International, Oxfam and global refugee charities. The actual list of activist support groups she is involved with is a lot longer than her screen credits.

Lastly, because I love him, William Shatner, who played the dashing Captain James T. Kirk in the original *Star Trek* series and also has a heavy emphasis on Aries. In interviews he admits that Jim Kirk and he are so alike and he is simply himself in that role. Hence we see leadership, courage, battle skills, and, of course, a defender of human morals.

Aries, as a "me first" and Masculine-oriented, pioneering energy, likes to be at the helm of the ship. Ariens dislike taking orders and coming under the rule of others. If so constrained, then the temper and critical impatience will quickly overrun the warm charm we see if everything is going well.

While living in London, I knew an Aries Sun headmaster who took in all the children that the more middle-class schools around would not accept. The children might have been expelled from another school for bad behaviour, or they were refugees and spoke no English, or didn't have shoes to put on their feet, and he would rise instantly to the challenge, making more space in his overcrowded classrooms, ignoring all the horrified middle-class parents who then removed their children in droves. This headmaster also chaired the headteachers' union, and championed the causes of protecting teachers from government bureaucracy and performance-linked pay rises.

Let's be plain-speaking and say that Aries is no peace-seeker. Because Aries loves combat, it actually doesn't want life to become utopian and fair for all, because then there wouldn't be a fight any more, and this energy must have a battle. What use is a soldier with a sharp and mighty sword if there is no battle to fight?

Another potential drawback: Aries is not a team player. The energy is about its own need for victory, prowess, and glory. Ariens cannot give this up for team stuff unless they can be leader, then they excel—at leading. Not, however, at the diplomatic and patient handling of the workforce.

Aries energy is difficult to live with if you are an underling. Ariens can be short-tempered with those closest to them (or even those not close to them). The Aries temper is quick and sharp if a certain standard isn't reached. It is possibly another excuse for a crusade, this time on the side of perfection and against slower mortals or perceived sloppy workmanship. But it can be very hard to live with.

Irritability and nastiness become even more apparent if Aries is not using the Arien energy in a constructive and useful way. For instance, if a strongly Aries character is employed as a library assistant, then this pent-up, frustrated warrior energy will not have an authentic and dignified outlet. Oh dear.

When Arien energy becomes disproportionate it becomes brutish and bullying. Excessive or frustrated Aries energy can also vent itself on the body of the Arien character through headaches, raging fevers, accidents with sharp metal, or burns.

Aries is sporty, most especially in anything competitive in the "sword/racquet wielding" category, such as fencing, squash, or badminton. The planetary ruler of Aries, Mars, has been proven to be a significant energy in the charts of athletes in general. You can always spot the Aries-led soccer or rugby player, since they are the hot-headed ones who take part in a battle not only with the other side but with the referee as well!

Interestingly, Aries won't show vulnerability in the heat of battle, so when an Arien soccer player throws himself on the floor in supposed agony it is done as a flamboyant showy part of the game; he wouldn't naturally show his pain at that point. Much more natural to the Arien is rugby, where you're a sissy if you flinch at your broken collarbone and leave the battle before half-time. But once off the battlefield Aries becomes the cry-baby who needs his mother.

With all this zealous love of battle, you would expect Aries energy to be bad at losing, but Aries can be strangely chivalrous if the opponent is recognized as not a fair match for Aries's superior battle tactics. So little children are allowed to win board games. If, on the other hand, the opponent is well matched or bigger—such as His Majesty's Government—well . . . Aries doesn't lose under these circumstances, it just keeps on fighting!

Fire has a Masculine, pioneering spirit and Aries energy typifies this in its need to lead, initiate, and instigate. Because its primordial instinct is to spring into life from the undifferentiated mass that precedes life-as-we-know-it, it boldly leaps forward and leads the way. Hence Ariens act like natural leaders and attract leadership roles as a result. It is a pioneering need to be in the front or at the helm, calling, "This way" to the troops behind them. Remember this energy is simple, direct, and uncomplicated. They aren't actually motivated by the pay cheque either; if a job offers absolute autonomy with no interference, they will take that role rather than the higher-paid one that defers to a monthly committee. The "me first" impulse is far stronger than the longing for more money, which Aries happily lets others have.

When money is involved, some people resort to cunning and subterfuge; this is confusing for Aries energy, which is much more straightforward. They often don't see deception coming, and Aries's financial naivety can be abused by the more manipulative and secretive predators. Aries energy is not helpless or stupid, it just cannot be deceptive itself, and therefore doesn't suspect it of others. Don't forget Aries doesn't think much about others' motives—Aries is very much absorbed with its own impulses, and doesn't get as far as the impulses of others.

So add this innocent belief in others' motives to the Aries tendency to save the lame dog, and you can see how Aries becomes a very soft touch. Ariens are great people to borrow a tenner from, since they often don't ask for it back! Money isn't that important, so Ariens may give generously to friends—which leads me to say that they just don't help themselves sometimes.

Such is the Aries impatience with detail and money that Aries is extremely bad at handling things like Inland Revenue accounts. And when you consider how many of them are self-employed, then this must be an irritating issue for a lot of Aries-led people.

Romance is interesting, since Aries loves to be in love and rushes in headlong without thinking, particularly if a hard-to-get chase is involved. If not, it can rush out just as quickly! When in love, Aries is romantic and faithful. Capable of great tenderness . . . for a while. But once Aries has chased and finally captured the object of desire, they can get bored and need more stimulation. Where Aries energy is present, there needs to be a lot of dynamic rushing around; if you don't make sure there is lots of sport and action, there will be trouble.

A bored Arien energy becomes extremely irritable and crotchety. The pettiness and unreasonableness, backed up with a violent temper, is best avoided at all costs. It is sensible to keep Aries on the crusading, pioneering, sporty path—and therefore employ a cleaner, gardener, and accountant if things do progress to wedded bliss and domesticity. This makes for a calmer, less stressful life.

An Aries weighed down with boredom will seek to relieve it by going into battle with the lawnmower—or you, yelling and shouting at you for doing "nothing" while they do "all the work." You cannot argue with this, you cannot point out the washing up, nappy-changing and laundry-drying that you have done—they don't see that; it's all detail; and anyway a battle is required and you'll do!

It has to be said that a strongly Arien nature is harder for females than males when it comes to living together, domesticity and childrearing. A male will join a squash club and not come home; she can only seethe, smash plates, and rage when he doesn't—and then do the same when he does!

An Arien woman desperately needs the same kind of challenge to push against that a man needs, and baking cookies for the cake sale and shopping for the cheap offers in a supermarket does not provide this. So, she becomes trapped, miserable, extremely irritable, and bossy. It would probably be easier to consider childcare so that her leadership strengths and dynamic and pioneering skills can be given the appropriate outlet at work. Because she is a whirlwind of greased lightening, she could easily cope with the housework as well. Taking her out of the commercial or business world for 15 years or so might mean she cannot achieve the senior position that she is truly capable of taking.

An interesting feature of Aries people is that they rarely gossip. Firstly, others aren't that interesting; Aries is a self-centred Sign after all. secondly, gossip requires subtlety and care with what one repeats to another, and Aries can't be bothered with that. And thirdly, they are kind of protective of their friends, so they don't like to call them names or discredit them. However, their friendships tend to work best when they are the leader.

Lastly, Ariens hate dentists—after all, it's not a fair battle. The dentist is holding the sharp, pointy thing and Aries is not allowed to leap up and defend itself with another weapon. Aries-type people secretly hate pain and can be real cry-babies with toothache, migraines, and headaches, which they can get more than most. Because the Element of Fire acts from the gut (gut instinct), they also seem to get stomach and intestinal disorders if their Fiery nature is blocked—the Fire starts burning the gut. Like all Fire signs, Aries is guilty of ignoring the well-being of the body, and although Aries loves sport, it is not for health reasons.

~ LEO ~
Fire Zodiac Sign

Glyph ♌
Fifth Sign of the Zodiac Belt
Middle Fire Sign
"I will"
Ruled by the Sun
Symbol is the Lion

This chapter does not refer to Leo as a Sun sign but to the Leo energy that exists in all of us to a degree. Leos or the Leo types discussed here simply have more of it than most.

"I am as I am, my own special creation"—these lines from a song remind me so much of Leo. There is a play on the word "pride" since Leo is ruled by the lion and a lion has a pride of females; but also, being proud and having pride are very Leonine attributes.

However, this is the middle of the Fire signs and, as with the middle sign of all the Elements, Leo often bears a great deal of pain while also being noted for such gifts as humour, and an ability for dramatic entertainment.

Leo is about the need to feel special, unique, and important. We need to feel a sense of our own importance in order to love ourselves, and want the best for ourselves. We then have confidence in our ability to decide for ourselves, to know how we want to express ourselves, and how we want to be creative, to laugh, to love, to enjoy, and to play.

But in striving for these things, we learn the pain of being denied this self-expression. For to exhibit ourselves, to shine as brightly as we can, is to be flamboyant and attention-grabbing, and this will attract those who want to deny us that, and crush our need to be special. We then have to be bold enough to shine anyway, to not allow the pain of disapproval to dim our light.

During our childhood and adolescence, parental admiration, attention, and praise should make us feel admired and special. I call this "red love" and our Leo, in particular, needs it. There have been a number of academic studies that show a strong correlation between parental admiration and a child's future achievements and happiness. I am not accusing parents of not loving their children; but it is **the colour they love in** that has such a detrimental effect. This is discussed elsewhere in the book, but the repetition is worth it. Parents can love in blue with big concerns for the health and welfare of their child, but telling them to keep washing their hands will not encourage self-esteem. When a parent looks at a child with admiration in their eyes, something more than special is passed to the spirit of that child. And it grows.

We seek peer group approval at school. We want to shine. We want to be liked so we can feel good. And when we are not, when the other children are cruel and when our parents don't seem to admire and praise us, those with prominent Leo energy feel the intense inner pain of rejection, bewilderment at failure to be approved of, and the devastating feeling of being unloved and therefore unable to shine importantly.

Because Leo must get attention, it tries to get a sense of self-esteem by being important to others, by inflating and demonstrating its significance. Like a regal lion roaring through the jungle, demanding he be listened to. And this is where it all goes pear-shaped, because the more Leo strives hard to be liked, the more Leo is then seen by others as overly dramatic, overbearing, arrogant, and self-centred. Poor Leo is tormented and hurt, and cannot understand this lack of appreciation. Underneath Leo craves love and affection, and is not just thrilled by adoration and praise, it feels starved without it.

So, Leo will then set about different attempts to be liked and admired, and generally finds that humour works best. Leo has a heart as big as a bucket, and soon learns that a generous, magnanimous, and larger-than-life, loving approach is appreciated by the audience. And with the Sun as its ruler, no zodiac sign can make you feel more special as you bask in all that radiant warmth.

Really? You'd think that, as Leo is motivated to express Leo first and foremost, Leo wouldn't acknowledge those lesser mortals around it, but Leo energy loves affection and praise so much, it is willing to give it generously in return for an adoring appreciative audience. Leo can be extravagant with money and compliments, which are delivered so directly and openly it leaves the recipients dazzled and stunned by the generosity and warmth. The Leo energy wins people over just as easily as it can repel them. They can light up a room with their friendly hospitality and BIG personality.

Sometimes they are like the royal and noble king, lovingly handing out generous gifts of approval to the minions, and then enjoying a captivated and loving audience in return. However, let's hope the minions have tolerance and understanding, for royal disapproval and sudden overbearing actions can be equally stunning! The roaring of the lion can be unhesitatingly brutal.

When the lion loses its temper and starts rampaging round the jungle, there are a couple of tips to remember: it is not a brooder, and the not-talking-to-you moods that the Water signs go in for are rare. It is all over relatively quickly. This can be helped by appealing to its pride—Leo is unbelievably and quickly appeased by flattery!

Do try this out one day, and you'll be utterly amazed. I think it was Linda Goodman in her Sun signs book who first suggested it. I have used it ever since and it still works. Just as the roaring is in full swing, say something like, "Gosh, you are so powerful and mesmerizing when you get angry, it makes your eyes flash, you could be a god!" Seriously, you can be that ridiculous.

The lion will stop in mid-flow, the jaw will drop, then close, there will be a huffy final word, such as, "Don't think I am going to forget this" or, "Don't think I don't know what you're doing," and shortly afterwards, "Do you think so? I guess I've always been quite wise . . . you are very wise yourself . . . " (Always one to generously hand out magnanimous comments to others!)

Leo vanity is something else. This energy loves posing in mirrors, for even attention to self affirms its existence. The phrase, "Because I'm worth it" springs to mind, and positive Leo energy certainly thinks itself worthy! Leos will adorn themselves richly, with flash and style. The colours of flames are attractive to them, and red features a lot. Note how many strongly Leo-type characters drive a bright red sports car. They don't so much drive them as wear them. Ha! Now the lion feels properly robed. Even if red colours are not in evidence, impact will be. Maybe a big hairstyle, long and curly like a lion's mane, or maybe lots of jewellery. Madonna and Marilyn Monroe both have prominent Leo in their birth charts.

So . . . Leo is sensitive to image, appearance, and popularity, while hating criticism. If you were to point out the egg on the front of a shirt, or the blackcurrant stain on a sleeve, they would impatiently brush at it as if they could eradicate the blemish with one quick swish and so return the audience's attention to Leo's radiant presence.

A key feature of Leo is a strange eccentricity, which is born out of its far-reaching creative vision (which sees things differently to other zodiac signs) and its need to be itself. This means being different from the crowd, and not conforming to mainstream views. To be the same as everyone else is near-death to Leo, who must be individual above all else, even if this means being criticized. He'll brush aside or not hear the criticism, as cutting as it is; so long as he is different! (Leo is paired with Aquarius and it is the same for Aquarians.)

Leo energy is not subtle, for how does the Sun shine subtly? You can hide the strong rays behind clouds, but when it peeks out it is fully there, there is no dimmer switch to turn it down a little; and this is the same with Leos. They are all or nothing, black or white, no subtle greys or middle ground. You get the full hit or they are not themselves.

Leos do not understand warnings about being overbearing, or requests to be quieter. How can they be quieter? Less obvious? It's impossible. To tone it down is to snuff themselves out, and this is not what Leo was born to do. Attention is all.

As a Fire sign, Leo is romantic and visionary, seeing the huge potential and colourful possibilities in life, with stories, creative imaginings, and playful, fun-filled opportunity. If a real story is too boring, Leo simply embellishes it and adds colourful extras for more impact. It hates a drab ending. As a result, everything Leo says can be halved or doubled! The paradox is that they dislike things that aren't straightforward and clear-cut.

Leo's "lies" are likely to be exaggerations rather than manipulations. They will also lie to get themselves out of trouble, but they don't lie terribly well, and can easily be caught out.

This is the sign of love, BIG love, with all the passion and thrill of the gallant suitor with flamboyant declarations and hugely romantic gestures. As you can imagine, it is hard for Leo to hold back on something that seems so exciting and new.

Leo is a loyal and honourable sign in love. Leos are sensitive to the pain of others in as much as they have suffered so much themselves when cruelty has hurt them, they don't wish this to happen to anyone else. They can be exceptionally loyal and supportive when they perceive pain in others.

However, because Leo is a self-centred energy, they can unwittingly seem very uncaring and insensitive. I know of one Leo male who turned to his female companion as it began to rain and asked for the coat she carried. Thinking he would place it round her shoulders, she handed it to him. He thanked her, put it over his own head, and walked on!

This same Leo male took out health insurance for himself and not his wife when they reached their sixties, claiming that they couldn't afford two, and he had to come first as he earned the money! He didn't mean to be insensitive, he truly thought he was more important.

This also demonstrates the idiosyncratic Leo approach to money. Leo energy is lavish and extravagant when it wants to be, and Leo-type people are known for their spontaneous generosity, but they also show a really inept and naive approach to controlling and budgeting. Leo cannot deal with finances and accounts; it hates the detail and the tedium.

Leo also wastes a lot by not looking after its possessions. Leo's environment is usually cluttered and disorganized, so things break and get lost. Leo-type people then get angry with the "thing" and blame it and their own "bad luck." They don't see that it broke because they didn't care for it. For all that Fire, they are notoriously lazy—think of lions lazing about on the savannah. So they hate tidying up and expect others to do it for them.

Inflexibility can be an issue. They are fairly fixed and married to their own ideas. The enormous willpower is difficult to oppose.

They often have difficult issues with the father. It seems as if the way a father's love is delivered is not in the style Leo wants it. Father may be away more often than Leo would like, or may not show appreciation and admiration in the way Leo needs it to be. If it is a case of being "a chip off the old block," then perhaps the father is Leonine too, so the stage at home simply wasn't big enough for two Leo personalities, both expecting the other to be the audience.

However, it seems as if Leo energy is better off hurting early, so that they can begin to learn that the best way to feel good is to learn to feel good about themselves. To give themselves the "red love" and heal their own inner child. They need to do this to gather their own sense of power, in preparation for the outside world.

Without a huge sense of personal power, they will become envious of the power of others and wonder where all those feelings of resentment are coming from. They have to develop a powerful drive for self-recognition; this is what Leo is all about. Lions have to find their own space and independence, creating their own lives.

Lastly the Leo energy commonly suffers from seasonal affective disorder. All Fire signs need the Sun, but Leos most of all, so they suffer during dark winters.

~ Sagittarius ~
Fire Zodiac Sign

Glyph ⚹
Ninth Sign of the Zodiac Belt
Highest Fire Sign
"I know"
Ruled by Jupiter
Symbol is a Centaur, shooting an arrow

This chapter does not refer to Sagittarius as a Sun sign but to the Sagittarius energy that exists in all of us to a degree. Sagittarians or the Sagittarius types discussed here simply have more of it than most.

It will become clear as you read this section that one thing is certain: when you have got to know one, the Sagittarius energy will be unmissable.

So, let's get this said right away. Few Sagittarians will care what I have written here, because there is only one opinion that counts—their own. In fact, it is quite likely that no Saggie-person will ever read this. So I am writing it for all the girlfriends of Sagittarian-type people who would love to know why they are as they are.

When you first meet them, you will probably think them extremely knowledgeable and superior. The males in particular have a godlike air to them. But after a while it becomes obvious that there are flaws in their assertions and they may not know what they are talking about. But such is their confidence, no one questions them.

Sagittarius energy is found in the higher echelons of politics; also the judges, law lords, and barristers of the judiciary system are natural Sagittarian types. Then there are the consultants of this world, who apparently also know everything.

The spiritual or metaphysical community attracts many who feel their wisdom should be shared. This is also the energy of preaching and religious dogma—the "holier than thou" attitude. This means that Sagittarius can either be "holier than thou," or resent "holier than thou" when they find it in others. (And how Sagittarius hates it in others—chuckle!)

Just looking at education for a minute, this is the sign of teaching and higher education. Imagine if you will, the lofty professors of universities. If you are learning, you are in Gemini energy; if you are teaching with confidence, you are in Sagittarius energy. This is the sign of confidence, this is where confidence dwells, and what a difference that can make to anything we are trying to do.

Sagittarius loves adventure and challenge because it is not afraid. It is almost impervious to fear. This energy sails very close to the wind and gets away with it. It takes chances, which pay off because the support of the Fire Element is behind it. This is Fire's highest sign and its most magnificent showcase. Here the spirit of adventure and challenge runs free, with all the impulse of the rash and bold.

This part of your birth chart is where you have the least worries of the whole zodiac. Nothing else, apart from the planet that rules Sagittarius, Jupiter, can make you feel as omnipotent and buoyant. It is about being invincible, bold, all-knowing, and irrepressible. Kind of like the God of the Old Testament really—appears in fire, is pompous and haughty, and assumes authority without doubt.

Jupiter, the largest planet in the solar system, rules Sagittarius, and that makes sense; Jupiter is the Roman name for Greek Zeus, the king of the gods with an ego to match.

Okay, so Leo has a prestigious "king of mortals" association, but Sagittarius is ruled by the king of the gods on Olympus; just a tad higher. Hence, Leo is not the highest or most influential Fire sign. Herein lies Leo's issues. The annoyance at not being that omnipotent. The vulnerability of not being as impervious as Sagittarius is. And then the issue of being second in line, a "middle child syndrome" perhaps.

While we are on the subject of Olympus and religion, we should bring in other religions as well and most especially the one-god religions of Christianity, Islam, and Judaism. These have a built-in hierarchy of pompousness and authority that appeals to the Sagittarian nature. With titles such as "His All-Holiness," "Your Eminence," and "The Very Reverend," you can appreciate that Sagittarius naturally gravitates towards the status. Well, that and the fact that you get to preach to others in a legitimate way.

But religions are something of an issue for strongly Sagittarian types. They will go through very big changes to their religious beliefs one way or another, as they search for the truth they know is out there. Or they will be ridiculously dogmatic in their chosen religion, so that they push away any possibility of doubt and change. You can see those types on religious channels in the USA. Then there are the ones who refute all the mainstream, organized religions and go for the esoteric, obscure, metaphysical, pagan, or pantheist variety.

Those who undertake the change usually do so because they find fault with the doctrine that is being preached to them. Sagittarius is looking for the truth. It has to resonate with them. It has to be revealing, transformative, enlightening, and powerful. It also has to be a journey, and a journey that never ends. More revelations, more enlightenment, more transformation, and then more searching. The Sagittarian journey can be of the mind or body, but the favourite is a journey of spiritual or religious beliefs.

Since Sagittarius is about wisdom and higher meaning, the early years of Sagittarian-type people don't go particularly well. They know a poor teacher when they hear one, and immediately rebel because this truth isn't right. This doesn't go down well in a lot of schools. The young Sagittarian type would do better if left alone with the internet. Then they will find the teachers they need to listen to and eventually they will teach themselves, because they love teaching. They have clever minds, high standards, superior intellect, and they will strive for excellence. However, learning isn't something they are keen to do, unless they sense they are listening to the best there is—then they can't get enough of it.

While they make good teachers initially, as they get older they get disillusioned with the teaching establishment. Eventually they find so many faults with it, they throw in the towel and seek the supreme and perfect answer, truth, or enlightenment somewhere else.

It isn't hard to find a rebellious Sagittarian; they are rebels by nature. They hate rules with a passion and will always refuse to do what they are supposed to do. They just don't like to be told to do *anything*.

It is said they love a journey, not a destination, but I am not so sure. There is a destination when we go on holidays and Sagittarius energy likes doing that, despite the destination aspect. Perhaps the constant stimulation of a flow of new experience is what matters. To keep discovering and experiencing. The Sagittarius symbol is that of an archer who shoots arrows and follows them. They land somewhere, so I think a destination is fine, so long as there is another one. You'll find Sagittarian types driving lorries, and moving from local deliveries to long-haul very quickly. Or they become travel agents to make the most of the free travel perks.

Strongly Sagittarian types don't usually qualify for long service awards; they tend to move restlessly and relentlessly on, because the grass is always greener in the next field.

Let's consider some interpersonal skills. Sorry to be blunt here—must be the Sagittarian in me—but the archer's listening skills are rubbish. They rarely listen to anybody else. They have selective hearing and, as someone else is talking, they switch off because they know it all already. They just wait for a gap in the conversation so they can then carry on their pontificating. Strangely, they won't follow a pointing finger either. Say you are trying to show them something on a map, so you point to the place while you explain. Have a look at their eyes, and they will not be looking where you point. They can't, because they don't do what anyone else asks them to. Following a pointing finger would be like taking guidance from somebody else.

Similarly, they won't listen to gentle hints or advice. Then, when you get frustrated and shout, they will become righteously indignant and say sniffily, "You don't have to shout, how could you talk to me in this way, I don't deserve it . . . " Even though they were ignoring you to start with.

Can you believe that satellite navigation in cars can give Sagittarius interpersonal "issues?" On the one hand, this can assist them on journeys, and they love journeys. But on the other hand, they don't like being told what to do! So, they normally turn the volume down and just watch the moving screen. This surely must be unsafe, but higher Fire has no patience with "safe;" if you are a god, you are immortal and will live for ever. And just to appease any feelings of servitude at having to take instructions from "that woman" (as I heard one say) in the device, they then rant at how "wrong" and "inferior" it is. This helps them establish a feeling of superiority over the situation. I suspect this trait might be found in Aries and Leo too—let me know.

They will tell you they have fantastic memories, and they might do for things that interest them, but normal detail is not retained as a matter of course. Their lives are about the future, not the past, but also it won't suit them to remember things where they were wrong and you were right. Most of all, they can not be proven wrong, because that is "death" to them. They cannot survive that. So, their best defence is to forget or not remember. Then they are never wrong. They ignore their own mistakes. They just don't count somehow. They brush over them and become VERY resentful when reminded of past errors.

So, taking into account the self-selective memory loss and unreliable listening skills, do Sagittarian-types have many friends? Well, yes, in fact, they do, because as friends they can be interesting. They are spontaneous, larger than life, and fun to have around. But all that Fire is hard to contain. Some, particularly those with a Sagittarius ascendant, will wave their arms about or poke you to make a point.

They might crash your personal space with inappropriate actions, or try to plant a big kiss on the cheek of someone who would prefer to keep their own space.

However, their excitement is infectious and they will be the life and soul of any party. Watch them jump up to be first on the stage at an open microphone night. Fire loves performing and is fun, even without the stage. Their spontaneity can brighten dark winter days, but might be a little annoying if they just turn up at your door with no previous warning, as some like to do . . . "Surprise!" There you are, in a pair of very old and embarrassing pyjamas, lank hair, and last night's dirty pots spilling out of the kitchen sink. At this point, you could murder their spontaneity.

Those of us with a good helping of Fire in our birth chart love a challenge and the thrill of danger. Sagittarian-type people are real daredevils, enthusiastically leaping into anything and quite often getting away with it. If endless optimism can truly change the course of fate, then this is the energy to envy. However, the endless optimism can

43

be to the exclusion of plain reality, so they will make outrageous or naive statements about expected positive outcomes that just aren't possible. Like standing in middle of a hurricane saying, "It'll be fine in an hour or two, you mark my words." They make grand, BIG statements, backed up with a superior air of knowledge. Theirs is the boundless faith in tomorrow, for, despite all evidence to the contrary, they naively expect everything to turn out right.

Perhaps now is the time to think about how Sagittarius energy takes to romantic relationships. After reading so far, you may have an inkling of what I am about to say! The good news is that it all starts very well. Something novel and exciting is intoxicating to the seekers of new and thrilling experiences. As with Fire in general, Sagittarius energy rushes in with all the headlong passion of Zeus chasing a conquest on Olympus.

Here's the "but." But, as soon as it isn't new any more, Sagittarius starts to lose interest, and only the security-loving energies in the birth chart will keep that person in the relationship for the years to come. The problem is that Sagittarius energy needs a constant stream of new experiences and different horizons to aim for. So mowing the lawn or vacuuming is something akin to being incarcerated in Tartarus. To have to go over the same lawn or carpet once a week drives them crazy with boredom. This is a restless energy that must keep moving forward into different territory. To keep them by your side, you have to keep reinventing yourself, and always keep that little bit in front so they can't quite catch you. The relationship needs to be a mobile one that takes in a lot of travel and questing—but not beach holidays. This energy needs activity and multiple stops. Book all-action getaways, or they'll drive you mad pacing up and down the beach. These types don't lie down on a beach mat unless they are asleep; chilling out and contemplating another massage does not do it for them.

Marriage is not an attractive proposition, they might do it once while young, or even get trapped a second time, but that will be it. From then on, they have been there and done that—there is no chance of a third time. And actually, that might be the relationship that works best for them. A friend, travelling companion and general "fixer" makes the best mate for Sagittarius types. They have the usual slapdash approach to keys, belongings, and tidiness that all Fire signs have, so a fixer is useful for bringing up the rear to put all the chaos in order again. Live apart and then you won't have to be their housekeeper as well.

However, opposites attract, and Sagittarius energy can be captivated by an earthy type whose practical abilities are sorely needed, but their down-to-earth pragmatism will puncture Sagittarian dreams once too often. Now, if you remember, the archer hates their dreams being put down more than anything else, so it won't be long before another opportunity comes up and the "bitter and nagging" earthy partner is left behind.

Here is a strange one to watch for. Sagittarius energy has a real fear of going over something again. For instance, if lost in the car they will not turn round and go over that last bit again. There may be a couple of reasons for this. They cannot face the humiliation of their failure, and having to redo something means it didn't go right the first time. But also, this energy is meant to move forward, not back.

There are probably two reasons that Sagittarius energy doesn't insure something and runs the risk that it won't be damaged or lost. They like the challenge of beating the odds: "Aha . . . I didn't insure my car and I got away with it. Yes!" And also, they can be penny-pinching with small sums, while throwing away larger sums by not planning or managing sensibly. For instance, they will buy a £2,000 holiday and not shop around for the best price, but then avoid paying the travel insurance.

Their careless approach to purchases can drive Earth and Air energies to open-mouthed horror. Of course, Sagittarian types use gut instinct and snap decisions to buy something—what else have they got? Instinctive and fast-moving Fire is in charge. Careful planning or shopping around is not in the Fire toolbox, so they do lose money. They don't seem to examine or study any potential purchase; they glance and make a spontaneous leap. Going round and round on an internet search is not their thing; remember they don't like to go back over something? So comparing different websites is likely to cause rigor mortis.

Worse? They won't take bad purchases back. Remember? They don't go back. Perhaps they have big cupboards!

Like with Aries energy, Sagittarius also resents monetary obligations to government, local council, or state coffers, and likes to evade paying wherever possible.

Things tend to "spill out" of the strongly Sagittarian. They can't keep a secret and they are terrible liars. Saggies are basically friendly, and don't mean any harm, but don't tell them anything you don't want the world to know. Not having the refined or reserved genes, they tend to blurt out the things you would really rather they didn't say. The phrase "Rushing in where angels fear to tread" has a resonance here. Their spirit and their exuberance are bigger than their material body, so they find it difficult to operate—they "spill out" of it. To them, it is a nuisance and they don't know where it starts and ends—literally; their body spatial awareness is weak. Hence, they are clumsy and bang their heads a lot.

They don't go in for pretence and deception, and I think that is because they see it as unnecessary. First of all, they don't know how to rein back and be thoughtful—that's all too pernickety and detailed—but secondly, they believe in themselves so much, they can't understand why you wouldn't hang on their every word, no matter how ill thought out or blunt it is. They are confident enough not to care what you think, so they don't feel the need to carefully phrase things to impress the listener.

However, criticism—now that is a whole different ball game. They cannot stand criticism and get blisteringly angry. This is Jupiter, King of Gods, and you do not criticize the Almighty. Sagittarius thinks of itself as divine genius, and could not bear to think otherwise. Criticism is for mortals with all their failures, Sagittarius is divine, immortal energy and cannot be wrong. Question this and they will erupt into a violent temper. They aren't moody, but they sure are volatile!

The Element of Earth

Taurus · Virgo · Capricorn

Fig. 7: The Earth Signs

We have learned all about the Fire Element with its three signs, and now we are going to introduce the first astrological "conflict" and study the Element that is "opposite," the Earth Element.

This is similar to thinking about the diameter of a circle. The two ends of the straight line that bisects the circle are the furthest apart they can be, and yet the line reminds us that they are connected, they share contact, and there is a journey between the two. We are looking at the dynamics and psychology of "opposition" in astrology.

The opposition has more potential for frustration, learning, and eventual spiritual growth than any other formation. Something can be gained; there is a basis for understanding, if not admiration. So let's dig in . . .

It is important to note that Fire and Earth are terrified of each other. Fire is frightened of the orderliness of Earth and Earth is horrified by the disorder of Fire. If a spectrum is a scale with an extreme at each end, then Fire and Earth are at each end of a spectrum.

However, the seed of one is in the other. Einstein was perhaps the first modern physicist to demonstrate a relationship between energy (Fire) and mass (matter/Earth) with his famous equation $E=mc^2$. And since the 1990s theoretical physicists have described quantum field theory, in which "odd excitations" and "invisible field energy" is common. For our purposes, all we need to understand is that it seems that matter (Earth) is made up of energy (Fire). This explains the animosity between Fire and Earth. At any moment, there might be a Big Crunch (as opposed to the Big Bang), and all matter could disintegrate into energy (Fire) once more. So Earth fears being turned into the chaos of

47

Fire once more, and Fire fears finding itself trapped in the structure of the material world.

Fire loves what it does not know and what cannot be seen, while Earth loves all that is material, known, familiar, and therefore trustworthy. It likes to make something predictable out of the available, not dream up what could be, if only.

There are so many words that can be used to describe Earth—solid, reliable, practical, dependable, realistic—and all of them are reassuring in an earthy way. This is all about the comfort of status, money, and security.

We are now in the world of the Feminine polarity, so movement is much slower, therefore passive and reflective. So how does Earth defend itself? It isn't particularly assertive, but it will hold on when security is threatened. This Element has strength of endurance and persistence. It is cautious and premeditative in matter-of-fact, sensible ways, to make sure nothing is taken from it. Earth Element people run their lives with common sense and don't take risks.

I like the phrase "down-to-earth," which is so completely accurate astrologically, but also means realistic, unpretentious, and being concerned with practical actions and practical things. But there is yet another reason it amuses me—these guys are literally good gardeners. As long as they are aware they are, or have a self-recognized love for it, plants respond. In the UK we say they have "green fingers."

Now, it is possible to find a Taurean Sun sign who won't even have a house plant in their environment, but this is when another Element is suppressing Earth's expression. And that is what we are going to learn: how to tell when the Elements and their signs are being thwarted, leaving a budding gardener declaring they "hate" plants.

Earthy people will instinctively tidy and they "tend," as in take care of, watch over, look after, or attend to. I was at the party of a two-year-old girl recently. I was aware that she had a Capricorn Sun sign and a Taurus ascendant (which she had inherited from her Taurus Sun mother). Before her was a pile of nicely wrapped birthday presents. Now, what would Earth energy do with them? Fire would have had the wrappings off before I had the time to type this, and the room would be covered in the results of that enthusiasm. Not so this little

Earth princess. Each present was carefully opened as she peeled the sticky tape slowly off the paper. And after each present was opened, she collected up the paper and put it into a waste-paper bin. You get the picture. Even at that early age, an overdose of one Element will shine through. Heaven help her future partner.

Earthy people, as we might expect, keep their eyes firmly on the ground in front of them, taking carefully measured steps. After all, it is earth that infuses them. The problem with this is, they might never see the sky. Never look at that wide-open expanse and imagine the possibilities. Fire looks up for inspiration, Earth looks down. Okay, that's great if you are a farmer and understanding earth will earn you a living. But if you aren't tilling the land and work in an office instead, then you may not be able to see your way out of a boring job. In which case you can get locked into drudgery or even unhappiness; there is no escape because "Life is like this."

Earthy people love rules and form and they can be pessimistic to the point of dragging things down with lack of faith and optimism. What Fire sees as a prison, Earth enjoys as a safe place. They like to know where the boundaries are, so they can stay safe within them, and they will rigidly apply rules if required. You know the sort—a long intake of breath, a shaking of the head: "Tut, tut, tut, not on my watch, mate! Them's the rules, no paper ticket, no entry."

Unfortunately, too much Earth will lack in joy, freedom, and hopefulness; it is all about labour and routine. Take Earth to its extreme and it's all about miserliness, or the amassing of so much money it cannot be enjoyed. The character Scrooge in *A Christmas Carol* is a good example of an overly Earthy person. Despite having considerable personal wealth, he underpays his poor clerk Bob Cratchit and hounds his debtors relentlessly, while living cheaply and joylessly. Like the little girl opening her birthday presents so neatly and tidily, Scrooge doesn't know how to play.

There has to be a good side, right? And there is. They can enter a realm of feeling that no one else can reach. But this isn't the "feeling" of emotions, it is the feeling of sensations. They relish the senses, they are sense-ual. They delight in the olfactory sense of smell, the gustatory sense of taste, the auditory sense of sound, the somatosensory sense of touch through the skin, and finally the sensory stimulation of vision. The Earth Element resonates with this network of neural structures that is a subset of the sensory nervous system. The upshot of this?

They feel at home in their bodies, they understand the thousands of unconscious messages the body sends the brain. Their sensory perceptions keep them informed of where they are and how they feel, and in touch with the beauty around them. They access the information that a person made of too little Earth Element (or too much Fire Element) simply won't get.

If Earth is found in the right place in a birth chart, then that person will likely be involved in hands-on-body therapies like massage, physiotherapy, osteopathy, occupational therapy, or any career that appreciates and refines the body, like fitness trainers and beauticians.

I should imagine that a great many carers and nurses are Earthy, because Earth is comfortable with illness and the needs of the body. It is also successful with discipline, hard work, long hours, patience, and dependability.

They can also build the dreams of Fire into reality. Earth looks hard at Fire's scantily clad visions, sighs, picks up the baton, and slowly puts order to them, thoughtfully, realistically, and practically. They give the dream, form. We are in "Feminine" energy and Earth is generally muted and steady, rarely claiming attention for its achievements, so Fire can bask in the applause for the brilliant idea that would never have made it without Earth.

Earth will wait and grow its coffers shrewdly and wisely. Since money is a measurement of value, and Earth is all about understanding worth and protecting it effectively so that it can grow, Earth is the money-making Element. Earthy people usually demonstrate an effective building of assets, from pensions, savings, and homes to a good stash of chocolate in the sweet or candy cupboard.

It is quite common to hear Earthy people declare that they "don't believe in woo-woo or hocus-pocus," the spirit or soul surviving death and psychic powers. Astrology and other dimensions will have to be "proven" before Earth accepts such things are possible. However, once Earth does believe in these things it will stick to the new belief.

~ TAURUS ~
Earth Zodiac Sign

Glyph ♉
Second Sign of the Zodiac Belt
First Earth Sign
"I am"
Ruled by Venus
Symbol is traditionally the Bull,
but we should include the Cow too.

This chapter does not refer to Taurus as a Sun sign but to the Taurus energy that exists in all of us to a degree. Taureans or the Taurus types discussed here simply have more of it than most.

Taurus is the first of the Earth signs and, as such, plants itself very firmly into existence with an uncompromisingly stubborn attitude. Taurus says, "I am here to enjoy the natural and material pleasures of this dimension; that which is corporeal and solid in form."

This love of form means that Taurus doesn't appreciate any mystical, intangible, or psychic phenomena. Nor are they fans of astrology or the quantumly weird.

Our bull/cow people have to hold and feel things, then they are "real." They themselves are solid as a rock if pushed. They value simplicity and basic facts because subtle and complicated is too . . . complicated. Earth is the opposite Element to Fire, so it is more fixed and persistent than Fire.

Taurean-types have a real appreciation of luxury and blissful sensations, one of which is taste; they really savour home-cooked and comfort food. I'm thinking here of the smell of fresh bread, or a meat/cheese pastry straight out the oven. Maybe a fine wine, or sweet strawberries and cream. They relish all the senses, but they particularly delight in the senses of smell and taste. The zodiac sign of Taurus clearly rules the tongue, or that part of the tongue which reacts to rich, sweet tastes and a luxuriant mouth-feel. So, Taurean types are just so good at identifying the best food and drink.

Now, having said *all* that . . . I'm going to lay the ground for the exceptions. There are a few Taurus types who prioritize perfect physique over eating. These are the gym types who worship at the altar of a beautiful body and so deny themselves culinary pleasures. They also preach to others about the dangers of overeating. Because they are so stubborn, they can keep a vice-like grip on their punishing exercise routine and meagre diet. And there are none so obsessed than those whose dark side harbours a famished soul who would rather eat a mountain of cheesecake than one more lettuce leaf.

Generally speaking, obsession is always funded by a hatred of that very monster within, although its existence is always denied.

Let's not forget the Taurean fine eye for furnishings, art, and quality materials such as solid oak and marble. Taurean types love value and solid durability in the things around them. If possible, buildings and cars should be built by craftsmen from superior materials. Taurus would rather wait and save patiently for the best than quickly get something cheap and less substantial.

They love antique and the traditional, even if that material has gone out of fashion. They know its superiority over plastic makes it worthwhile in the long run. Gold jewellery is not lost on them. This is the sign of money, wealth, and value, as in "value-able" and valuable. Taurus seeks, builds, and creates things of value with a slow but steady drive and fixed, sustainable energy. They set realistic targets and plod steadily towards them, leaving over-ambitious dreams for the Fire signs. In the Taurean world, potential is measured and achievable.

Let's look at the type of thing that catches the breath of a Taurus-ruled person. Unsurprisingly, property, land, and buildings are sought after and invested in, rather than speculative things that can't be seen and touched. Claims of big gains and investments that rely on speculation and chance, like the futures market or hedge funds, are not the sort of thing the bull/cow goes for.

Going back to their sense of touch, it is possible that females find it easier to identify with soft fabrics like velvet, silk, and cashmere. They also like their environment to be richly and warmly decorated, with no expense spared. Because of the body's sensitive nervous system, beds must have soft mattresses and, ideally, Egyptian soft cotton sheets.

Or—and here is the paradox; because they are earthy and nature-loving, they are happy to live in a roughly hewn forest hut, where they forage for food and collect hens' eggs from the small flock. The beds can be piles of straw and the water is drawn from a well. So where are the physical beauty, luxurious fabrics, and beautiful music now? They are still there in the glorious scenery, the birdsong, the carpet of soft moss, and pink sky of Sunrise. The solid and predictable Earth with its dependable seasons and constant affirmation of eternity and abundance. This is the Taurean promise: the material world (Gaia) will replenish and secure us for ever.

The Taurus in me asks where this promise stands now, in the light of a heavily overpopulated, heavily destroyed environment. This needs to be addressed by the Taurus in each of us.

As a Feminine sign, Taurus does have a soft, gentle demeanour, but a fixed, solid, bull-like stance will be seen if defensive mechanisms are required. Taurus won't be pushed! However, when Taurus does start to move forward, and picks up traction, they can then be difficult to stop. Imagine moving a bull around and then you have it! The bull may be slow to rouse, but then go straight to full force. I have heard Taurean-type people called dogmatic and even fanatical. They do need to learn flexibility, and letting go of things is a problem.

Taurus, being a sign that represents Earthy values, can get wrapped up in its own views, values, and opinions. The dark side of this is intolerance, belligerence, and inflexibility. It's that fixed, dogmatic side of Taurus that hangs on to stuff without reviewing it. On the one hand, this is a loyal, unswerving, dependable energy. On the other, we encounter uncooperative stubbornness.

While we are looking at the dark or flip side of Taurus energy, let's make a note that love of food can become a greedy, rampant appetite or addictive compulsions. Unfortunately, Taurean self-centred and fixed determination to have what it wants doesn't help.

Along with the other Earth signs, Taurus wants social and relationship "form" and security too. There must be a formal first date, an engagement with a good ring, an expensive wedding, a honeymoon, a marital home and mortgage, a pension, and babies. All in that order.

They also like to make sure any potential partner has the right credentials. Are they a good provider?—there must be evidence of stability, reliability, and proper commitment.

Taureans can be quite possessive about their partners, and it is more about possession than jealousy. They protect and keep what is theirs. They are often good-looking and well-dressed themselves and they seem to prefer larger partners, possible because there is more of them. Bodies don't embarrass them—remember, they are generally at home with anything they can touch.

Males in particular struggle to understand complex emotional demands. One of the benefits of Taurus for them is the simplicity of black and white. They don't dwell in complex emotional quandaries and they are not into sexual or emotional blackmail. They can't really understand all that and don't see the need for it. Taurus seeks the basics: lots of physical pleasure, and their security needs met. That's it.

Taurus women have all the power of an Earth goddess or temple priestess. They combine practical skills with the prowess involved in pleasing men; skilfully wafting beautiful perfumes, silk lingerie, and home cooking . . . and all with sensual allure.

Expensive and valuable gifts are appreciated, both given and received. These are, after all, material possessions of value, which Taurus types treasure. Our bull/cow people look after and preserve belongings. To leave something behind is important and Taureans will put effort into this. Perhaps a building, but a form of art will do, such as a piece of beautiful music, a painting, a sculpture, or a landscape garden, built solidly with great determination and endurance.

As the first of the Earth Signs, Taurus is the first to celebrate the material world of matter. This is the "feeling" sign, but these feelings are not of the emotional kind; that is Scorpio's realm, the sign opposite Taurus in the zodiac belt. The "feelings" are the tactile, touchy-feely kind, with the skin being a very important part of this. Taurean types are pleasure-loving and they take that pleasure from the senses of the body; it is a "self"-centred energy. This is the sign of sensuality—but note that sensuality is not sexuality. It is true that Taureans enjoys sex, but the pleasure is derived from the sensations on the skin. The softness, the smell, the touch, the taste, and the pressure on the skin. The body is all important. Actual sex is neither here nor there.

They are most at home when they are in a warm environment with the opportunity to caress and feel things through fingers and skin. That can be a soft rug on the settee in front of a real fire, or it can be a spring day in the garden potting plants. So long as everything is peaceful, serene, languid, lazy, and opulent, the bull/cow is in clover.

Note: I am loath to leave the cow out of Taurean symbolism and I draw on the history of the bull and cow in Ancient Egypt as evidence. Please see the "Myth of the Heavenly Cow" and Hathor's cow ears at her Dendera Temple if you are not convinced. From my own experience, Taurus energy is resonant with cow-dairy products; it is quite often one extreme or the other—they are either much-loved or cause allergic reactions.

~ VIRGO ~
Earth Zodiac Sign

Glyph ♍

Sixth Sign of the Zodiac Belt

Middle Earth Sign

"I worry"

Ruled by Mercury, co-ruler Vesta

Symbol is the Maiden

This chapter does not refer to Virgo as a Sun sign but to the Virgo energy that exists in all of us to a degree. Virgoans or the Virgo types discussed here simply have more of it than most.

The Virgoan energy is opposite the sign of Pisces and together they make an opposition that concerns itself with "service." Virgo is the more junior sign and its service is devoted to domestic work, productivity, and service to individual humans.

As with the middle sign of all the Elements, Virgo is probably the most painful of the Earth signs. The other two signs are pretty sure of themselves, but Virgo rarely feels that confident. This is the energy that dutifully scrubs, tries to organize, works hard, dithers, and worries.

In fact, let's get all the anxiety issues out into the open first. In the context of the solar system (the name for the system of planets around our Sun), the Virgo energy has the unenviable task of trying to restore order to the chaos of Leo's Fire, which comes before Virgo in the zodiac belt. And, as if that isn't enough, poor Virgo also has to defend the Earth Element from the final dissolution of Water's Pisces energy. As I said before, Pisces is opposite to Virgo, and if you imagine Virgoan energy as the sandy beach, then the ocean's Piscean waves could crash up that beach at any moment, washing away all the sandcastles.

This reminds me of the goddess Ma'at in Ancient Egypt, who was the personification of "cosmic order." If Ma'at is doing her work properly then the material cosmos or solar system is held together in good working order. The flooding of the Nile, the planting of crops, and the yearly rituals had to be as regular as clockwork or their world would not hold together. So the goddess Ma'at was fundamentally vital, but so was the fundamental "order" of Ma'at, which meant balance, harmony, justice, and truth all rolled up together. The Egyptians strove to maintain the order of Ma'at, which I understand to be the balance between Fire and Earth.

And to be honest, Virgo's work is fundamentally vital too. Comparisons are often made between the sign of Virgo and Demeter, the Greek goddess of edible crops and harvest. In both of these we see the work that goes into the productivity of Earth, the weeding, the watering, the planting. Total service to productivity.

So, the focus here is how Virgo gives dignity and respect to humble service, and this is a really important point. It's great to be a flashy Fire Sign, but what actually makes it all work? Without Virgo, Fire's dreams cannot manifest successfully.

In Virgo-land, menial tasks are diligently and respectfully carried out with thoroughness; they delight in the true meaning of service. Virgo excels at secretarial service and problem-solving at the domestic level. Generally, they have good and reliable memories, and they are usually modest and earnest.

Virgoan people can be found working in the dental industry, health services, and service industries in general. They take messages, wash the cups up, switch the lights off, then grope their way to the exit in the dark, locking the building behind them. Security is always important.

They are such excellent workers, and natural employees. Generally, they are humble and self-effacing, so they don't want to be the boss. They like to stay in the background, fastidiously organizing after others and attending to the forgotten details. They love to make the tea, and take the minutes. They will look after the money from the charity collections—and who wouldn't want someone who is fastidious with accounts sorting their tax affairs out? However, this is a complex sign, often involved in painful human processes, as all these middle signs seem to be. Their great need, after being of service, is to be self-contained, which, of course, is completely at odds with the service gene.

For all the zodiac signs there is a great love or talent and with Virgo energy it is usually an obsession with health. So, healthy routines, healthy lifestyle, service to the body, medical issues, supplements, diets are all keen topics. I have known more than one walk around with a handbag like a medicine chest. They are fully equipped for first aid emergencies and often react well during such times, since they keep a clear mind. Their analytical skills can be useful in emergencies because emotional issues don't clog Virgo's clear view and practical, pragmatic, no-nonsense approach.

Virgo comes from a Latin word meaning maiden, which some take to mean unmarried. However, it is not as simple as that. It is about maintaining some separation, keeping oneself to oneself, and needing no one. Despite Earth's pleasure in the close proximity of others and the status that marriage awards, this energy needs to spend some time alone for inner focus. I think this is to do with their sensitive energy. They have a cellular "vibration" that is hard to maintain, and it requires separation in order to restore their equilibrium (or Ma'at!). Some of this anxiety is to do with the constant threat of annihilation by Fire or Water. It doesn't bother sturdy Taurus or Capricorn, but it sure rattles delicate Virgo.

Why so delicate? Astrological lore was being decided centuries before all the planets were discovered, so there were bound to be some discrepancies and this is one of them. It was decided that Air planet Mercury should be the ruler of the Earth Virgo zodiac sign. This hasn't been the best of "fits" and I think it has contributed to a limited understanding of Virgo. The mixed messages are confusing.

Possibly, Virgo's actual ruling planet, Vesta, was smashed up by major impacts at a time of turbulence in our developing solar system. Vesta had been a proto-planet like the Earth, with a crust and a core, but was reduced to small planet-sized lumps and thousands of asteroids and rocks in the asteroid belt by the devastation.

Now then, if you were a zodiac sign and your resonant planet was smashed up in this way, wouldn't you feel a little shaken? And I make no excuses for taking these science myths and weaving them into our spiritual, psychological, and astrological understanding of the solar system. If we are going to say that one bit of space has meaning, we have to accept that it *all* does.

Anyway, we are left with a sign that stresses easily with worry, anxiety, and nervous energy, driving everyone nuts! What Virgo energy needs most of all is separation, a focus, and a process, and it can get this via yoga or meditation. When the yogi closes the eyes, focusses on quiet breathing, and concentrates on the desired altered state of consciousness, a restorative process takes place.

Virgo is the last zodiac sign of the personal half of the zodiac and it instinctively knows it needs to prepare and process all the experiences of the previous five signs. Virgo energy needs to sort through the learning process in order to complete and make sense of it, in preparation for the "significant other."

Hence, they must dissect, reflect, and classify everything they encounter. But in doing this they can come across to others as being critical. Virgo would like it to be understood in the context of wanting to help people get things right. They see themselves and their comments as being helpful. The waitress needed to hear that, "The table hadn't been cleaned properly and the eggs were undercooked." The railway ticket collector needed to be told how they could "improve the service to rail users." Grandchildren should be told where they went wrong in their homework. Friends should be told how critical they are and how they could do better. Virgo sees it as a duty to put everybody right—but when you are on the receiving end the criticism can be very heavy and maybe hard to live with.

Yes, Virgoans do like to talk, and this they get from Mercury's co-rulership. Mercury is the Air planet of communication, and Air can be critical, because it is perfectionist. However, the combination of critical Air with critical Earth is like an avalanche. They can go round and round and round, like a hamster in an exercise wheel, endlessly talking over the same things—or, to their minds at least, evaluating everything critically and to infinity.

"Why did she say that? What did he mean? Shall I start looking for another job? Where shall I invest this money? What is going to happen to the economy? I don't think they have got this right. Why is my neighbour doing that? Do processed meats really cause dementia? What about salt?"

I have to quote astrologer Sue Tompkins from *Aspects in Astrology* here, because I think she describes Virgo brilliantly:

"Virgo believes that if you examine an issue for long enough, you throw out what is extraneous, synthesize what is left, then you are bound to come up with the right answer . . . Virgo is concerned with improvement of self . . . "

The detail gene, which can so irritate the Fire signs, facilitates the Virgoan need to categorize things and get them into understandable, logical places, ready for improvement.

Okay, I think that is enough said about being critical to achieve improvement; it is about time we looked at the Virgo energy and emotions.

Let's be clear: like all Earth signs, Virgoans don't do emotional closeness. Virgo has good observation skills, and listens closely to others. But this is so they can give practical advice, and it can be mistaken for emotional empathy. It is caring in a way; Virgo's thoughts are about how much improvement can be made if they just give a little advice. However, the distance Virgo has to be at to do this makes Virgo emotionally distant. Virgo dislikes close emotional demands. The Virgoan ethos is that too close means you "can't see the wood for the trees." Or you are "blinded by love." Earth, particularly Virgoan Earth, is practical if nothing else, and emotional closeness means you can't see clearly. So, Virgo needs to step back, or push back, to get a clear, unemotional view. This is hurtful for those who think they have found loving responses and closeness, and sometimes, the sudden emotional coldness, or cut-off, is painful for more loving Water energies.

Virgo helps in a practical way; everything has a purpose and is useful. Virgo equates help with love. And that's how Virgo types show it. By doing your accounts extra-specially carefully. Or giving you unsolicited "helpful" critical advice, when all you really needed was a big hug. Will a nice clean tissue do instead?

Now, let's discuss routines. Simply put, Virgo energy reacts sharply if routines are threatened. Routines are rituals and they are very reassuring to Virgo types. You might be suggesting a free afternoon tea at a posh hotel in London, but their immediate response is likely to be no, because they have to take the dog out at that time. This is a psychological defence mechanism, and woe betide the soul who threatens it.

The routines are safe places, where chaos and disorder can be stamped out or avoided. The more that Virgoans are threatened, the more the routines are important. Excessive Virgo energy might suggest obsessive compulsive disorder, where the routines get out of hand.

Virgo types are very curious and like to know what's going on. This can come across as nosy, but it is an attempt to hold back the chaos and disintegration that threatens them always. Everything is an attempt to control the potential tide of drowning. Virgo longs for inner peace and solitude. Virgo listens and takes in everything. Virgo looks round the net curtains at the neighbours and pays attention to gossip. Everything must be filed and compartmentalized for possible future use. This is the unspoken anxiety within.

There is a mythological association between the vestal virgins of ancient Rome, Vesta, and Virgo. The priestesses were required to leave their families when very young and serve at the temple of Vesta, which was at the centre of Rome and the spiritual centre of the Roman empire. However, they were probably not virgins but actually sacred harlots, the last vestige of the powerful female goddess energy Nut, who once ruled over the Feminine sky in Egypt. Patriarchy ruled by the time Rome was in charge, but they were sensible enough to make sure there was a token, highly revered Feminine presence . . . just in case.

So, human Virgoan goddesses reading this, hold your head high; you come out of a great lineage.

~ CAPRICORN ~
Earth Zodiac Sign

Glyph ♑
Tenth Sign of the Zodiac Belt
Highest Earth Sign
"I achieve"
Ruled by Saturn
Symbol is the Goat (originally with a fish's tail)

This chapter does not refer to Capricorn as a Sun sign but to the Capricorn energy that exists in all of us to a degree. Capricorns or the Capricorn types discussed here simply have more of it than most.

When I was teaching astrology in my home and we got to Capricorn, the students were in for a shock. I would make sure the room was cold and I didn't serve the usual hot drinks and cake. I would also tell them that, due to a plumbing issue, there were no bathroom facilities either. And to this day, they will probably remember how it feels to be in Capricorn energy!

The harsh conditions and denial of pleasures gave us a great start in understanding the taskmaster of the zodiac signs. The energy of Capricorn, which exists in all our birth charts, actually attracts hardship, bewilderment, and an aching discomfort that feels like a pebble in our shoe or a thorn in our side.

To Capricorn energy, life is a serious business, and it has to be mastered if you want to survive. And this is actually the point—here, the austerity, rejection, and harshness are a great training environment for learning the survival techniques and emerging victorious.

Capricorn energy starts working on us at a very early age in one of a range of different ways; perhaps by making us fearful that our needs will not be met, or that we don't have what it takes. We feel impotent, inept, and inadequate. We might be filled with the dread of a painful encounter. Possibly our elder siblings or other children might literally beat us up. Perhaps we suffered humiliation when we had to wear shoes with holes in, or we went hungry because there wasn't enough to eat. This sign is all about the hard facts of life, realism, and pain; but, additionally, Capricorn removes any tools or skills that we might have been able to use to fix it.

However, pain and gain are proportional and the pain we suffer will have an equal amount of gain on its flip side. But how wisely will you learn your Capricornian lesson? We can gain mastery by working with it philosophically, accepting that this is not an easy life and we will all suffer somewhere along the line. We can then return to the painful issues and work hard on an outcome different from bitterness and a remaining lifetime of fear. We have to work *through* these things, not run from them or deny them.

The trouble is that Capricorn can render us incapable and overly cautious, so we may develop a very entrenched defence system around our fear, including denial that it exists. In which case, we will have a very prickly internal issue that has the potential to erupt in unreasonable ways and is totally outside of our recognition or control.

We can't heal anything that hasn't first been felt (or felt again if it was previously buried). It has to come to the surface or we won't be able to acknowledge the emotions, embrace them with unconditional love, and finally process them carefully, so we forgive and they heal. Working through pain in this way will teach us how to gain mastery over it.

Capricorn is a higher zodiac sign and a "higher" experience. It comes with a lot of the "old soul" wisdom embedded in the Feminine from ancient times, so we should seek within the Feminine polarity for healing; and there, we will actually find it. For lo and behold, the answer lies in the opposite sign of Cancer. (The psychology of astrology is amazing!)

Aha! Opposite signs again. A recognition of the importance of opposition as a tool in the psychology of astrology will be very useful. It can deliver so much in terms of understanding, therapy, and healing. Basically, hidden in the heart of every sign is its opposite sign, and that is the antidote to the first sign's issues. The seed of one is in the other; therefore, the answer to Capricorn's harsh barrenness is the emotional bonding and mothering that Cancer is so good at.

So, the Capricornian lesson of hardship and impotency is best approached by giving yourself unconditional love and acceptance. That is, from yourself . . . to yourself.

If this is resonating with you, try this out. Find an old, pocket-sized teddy bear and love it as if it were your dejected inner child, or your broken heart. Be very gentle with your baby, for it has been badly treated and misunderstood. Validate its pain and humiliation by recognizing how very, very real it is. Quieten your Air mind and Fire intuition. Let your Water and soul talk to you. Then you will learn why and how you had to fail.

Our birth chart Capricorn placement can make it extremely difficult and bewildering to even begin the journey into success, but it is possible, with a certain amount of struggle, to build our greatest rewards and most solid achievements there . . . eventually.

Our Feminine souls are ready to work on this from very early on, but the problem is that the rapid growth of childhood into adulthood takes precedence, so Masculine Air/mind and Masculine Fire/spirit take command and lead, with competition and survival as the main strategies. We are just too "young." The soul's pleas become more urgent in our late twenties and early thirties. For some, this is the time of our greatest regrets and loneliness, a place we just can't see our way out of.

Capricorn is capable of bringing hardship and failure to us, but in time, if we carefully learn what is holding us back and why, we can overcome the obstacles and turn the lead into gold, and things will improve immensely as a result. But not before we have gone down into our own Underworld, been stripped of everything, and then found our way back out again. (See the Babylonian myth of Inanna.)

Okay, so now we have learned about the Capricorn energy that occurs as a minor matter in all our birth charts. But what about those who have an abundance of it? Well, basically, in a nutshell, strongly Capricorn types were born knowing that it is all going to be extremely hard work and we are here to struggle.

Let's say a Capricornian has asked the way to the pot of gold at the end of the rainbow. As it happens, we know where that is, and there are two paths that we can point out. One is a quick walk through a glorious meadow and there, the pot of gold is placed into the hands of the seeker. Amazingly easy.

The other path leads up a mountain into Himalayan-type cold. Bitter, howling winds whip the blood out of skin and freeze the bones. Next comes a valley filled with an inferno of flames and belching, poisonous smoke. The heat is almost unbearable. Finally, there is a bed of nails to walk across before the pot of gold is released.

So which road would you go for?

Bearing in mind this is a metaphorical example, those with significant amounts of Capricorn in their birth chart are likely to answer that they would take the challenging road, because they don't feel like anything belongs to them unless it's been worked hard for . . . seriously. They were born to accept hard labour in life. It comes naturally. In reality, they don't *like* to take the easy road, they want the one that gives them a challenge—but, and this is the important bit, they also want and expect to get the payback in time. There are two aspects to the Capricornian nature. Firstly, they want a challenge and hardship; the pot of gold isn't going to feel permanent without that. Secondly, there must be a pot of gold at the end of it. The bit when the lead turns into gold is essential, or they won't join in.

There we see the calculating and purposeful side of the Capricornian energy; they spot the potential opportunity for rich financial gain and turn towards it without revealing anything. This is the highest Earth sign and, as such, it takes Earth's appreciation of the material value of things to its ultimate potential. There is nothing flashy about this; Capricorn is a Feminine energy, after all. The hidden agenda, the quiet deal, the thoughtful weighing up of options; these are Feminine attributes.

If you look at a list of famous Capricornians online, there is nothing remarkable about them. Often very dutiful and hard-working, they can appear to be humble—but don't be fooled, because they will quickly remind you who is boss with an authoritative stare. They make good politicians, but also actors, can you believe? Maybe that has something to do with the hardship and knock-backs that aspiring actors face, and then the status that society awards those who have made it.

Because of Earth's slow, contained, and almost passive demeanour, Capricorn types can appear humble, unassuming, and unambitious, but nothing could be further from the truth. They are actually socially ambitious and seek achievement through hard work, and mastery of some kind.

They remind me of royalty with their patient, stoic expressions. A look that only really belongs to those who know they have nothing to prove, nothing to compete against, and no one to impress—because the rank and title does that. Queen Elizabeth II was known the world over for her serious, stoic, but passive expression, and she has a double whammy of Capricorn ascendant and ruler Saturn on the midheaven.

We have already talked about the royal blood of Leo and Sagittarius, and yes, that is textbook astrology, but, bringing in some shadow psychology for a moment: as the opposite Element to Fire, I think Earth has its own royal presence in its sign of Capricorn. There is something of the prestigious that appeals to this energy and it constellates towards superiority and elitism when it can.

Let's look at Prince William's wife, Catherine. Her mother moved Heaven and Earth to get her into the same university course as William and that certainly paid off for the both of them, as William and Catherine met and fell in love. The strange thing is that Catherine's Capricorn inheritance is heavily resonant with Queen Elizabeth's in a really close way.

Realistically? There would have been few girls in that large university who wouldn't have wanted to date Prince William. But her Capricorn energy nailed it.

So, is it that the Capricornian person waits, assesses, and plans to climb social heights? Or does it just happen to them? I think it is a combination of both; it happens because they are always alert to it. Be suspicious if it appears they are doing something that will not lead to social achievement, because it is unlikely. It is more likely that they are playing their cards very close to their chest and are even using diversionary tactics to hide their intentions, which is typical of Feminine behaviour.

In the past, when married women were less likely to have careers of their own, Capricornian-type females would gravitate towards the poverty-stricken medical student or bank teller. It is like a magnetic pull towards the money-earning potential. And she will accept a sparse courtship and a partner who works 80 hours a week, because she knows that one day, if she hangs on in there, she will reap financial and social benefits as a doctor's wife.

Or she might unconsciously find herself "in love" with the grandson of some ancient millionaire, so one day he will inherit all, even though he is penniless now. Capricornian lady will put up with the undignified and austere conditions surrounding this man, maybe even his abuse of some kind, because one day—it will pay off.

As you might imagine, they are not particularly romantic, until they have found The Right One. Romance won't give you social status, the right kind of partner, a large family home, and an impressive pension. But power and status are attractive to them, and *then* we see just how attentive and romantically alluring they can be. Expensive lingerie is now an express requirement, along with courtship jewellery and a marriage proposal in the most exclusive of surroundings.

Once respectability, status, and financial security are all sorted out, the rest of their life takes on a different emphasis; they can relax and reflect more on "meaning of life" issues. Then a wacky humour becomes much more evident, and their placid conviviality and warm wisdom emerges from within.

Okay, so they probably don't ever become frivolous, and maybe they will always dislike wasting time on something that is going nowhere. They still like achievable goals, even if it is a leisurely ten-year project in the second half of their lives, and are quite happy plodding slowly and patiently towards them. This is because Capricorn energy doesn't play with complete abandon like Leo or Gemini does. If they enjoy themselves too much, they feel guilty. Every move has to have a purpose or they feel depressed about the lack of productiveness.

Perhaps we should look into the Capricorn shadow, which can be at its blackest when they are teenagers. This is because the tools in the Capricornian teenager's toolbox do not match the psychological demands of growing teenagers who need to take risks to develop a personal identity, gain acceptance, develop confidence, and make commitments. To manage those developmental milestones requires a certain amount of Fire confidence, which may be at their disposal; but if it isn't, things are about to get tougher.

Teenagers are usually most concerned with the opinions of friends, but in the case of Capricornians their peers don't usually share the same values of studious hard work and a dislike of frivolity, so the young Cappie is easily labelled a "nerd" and bullied. Fear takes over and the teenager withdraws even further. A child who may have already been reluctant, timid, and struggling with peer group superficiality may sink into addictive substance misuse as a way of coping with, or rejecting, the demands made of them. Read astrology pages and you will be told, "They can be rebellious in their youth;" well, maybe that is true enough if using alcohol or drugs gives them courage, but that is only half the story.

Okay, let's move into the twenty-something years of Capricornian-type people. Now we have the deeply studious, aspiring professional, desperate to grow up, who knows that all will be well when they achieve those professional goals. Probably the teenage years didn't go so well, so Capricornians deliberately avoid any further relationship fumbling until The Right One appears. As mentioned earlier, this will be some-one who shares those materialistic dreams of building properties and pensions.

And the twenty-something Capricorn shadow? It is found in what they will put up with to achieve those goals. They will for now tolerate abusive or addicted partners, constant work, and sparse living condi-tions. The restrictive environment, the punishing career, or relation-ship with a damaged person is a hairshirt thing that they will carry for a while. There may be two reasons for this; the first is the drive to pit themselves against life's hard experiences, the other familiarity—because Capricorn learned to suffer as a child, they do it for the rest of their lives.

Lastly, the after-thirty Capricorn shadow. All that caution and prag-matism may well have turned into reticence and cynicism. They have learned to be suspicious and not show their hand until they know all of the other player's cards. This can manifest as sensible protection, or it can go too far and then you have deep mistrust and maybe a well-disguised paranoiac fear. This is a Feminine sign, and therefore retentive, with hidden grievances. They may resent paying tax and those who receive welfare benefits. Remember we talked about Ebenezer Scrooge and Christmas in the description of the Earth element?

By the over-thirty-year-old period of life, they may be hiding snobbishness and disdain. Capricornians are now finally achieving over their peers, so all the painful condemnation can now be paid back with interest.

Oh dear. For some, there may be no recovery from all those earlier hardships. They will assess in the negative and their milk bottle is half empty, not half full. The potential for it all to go wrong is always there for them and they permanently expect the worst.

Or, when they have charmed you into thinking how convivial they are, you may experience the gentle probing about your finances. This is subtly done, so you may not notice. However, Capricorn is assessing your wealth and financial status; if it doesn't amount to much, you will remain in their outer circle. These Cappies appear to be positive thinkers, but they are not going to associate with those who do not share their values and have personal wealth. Otherwise, further down the road, it may cost them money.

Let's look at some positives after all that. Capricorn types have high standards which are of great value in their chosen career, where they will improve industry practices with their strict standards. I would certainly buy a house built by one. They build with immense skill and determination and their homes will be in the best area they could afford. Schools will have been well researched, as will the good-quality car on the drive. I would also find their chosen charity shop, since they mostly wear quality clothes. They don't break their promises; this is important to their self-image.

As with the opposite sign of Cancer, family life is important; however, Capricorn is concerned with tradition and structure, while Cancer concerns are to do with nurturing, feeding, and unconditional love. Family and marriage commitments are taken very seriously and responsibly.

Cancer is associated with Mother, while Capricorn has old associations with Father. These were coloured by the nineteenth-century image of a stiff, authoritative, formal man whose standards were hard to live up to. Maybe that isn't so much the case these days, but it is worth enquiring about your client's relationship with their father, just in case.

Capricorns can be born into rich families because their parents pass down the Capricorn energy. Children inherit their parents' important signs. But how does that feel if you actually need to struggle? The soul will work from the unconscious to bring about the circumstances that will allow their Capricornian energy to be honed by challenge. No doubt the bewildered parents will say they gave them everything, so what did they do to deserve this? Keep up your astrology studies and one day you will be in a position to answer that question.

Spiritual matters usually arrive late, if ever, to the table of the Capricorn male. But in general it is not the same journey for females, who often turn to the metaphysical market. For them, a spiritual awakening is a matter of finding, from within, the emotional warmth and unconditional love that is Cancer's domain. Remember the seed of one is in the other? Cancer's emotional security completes the Capricorn lady, enabling and encouraging her to seek even more from her invisible self. As she becomes a rock for others to lean on, she feels the admiration and her Fire/spirit grows in response.

The sensible, strong, earthy Capricorn lady is now at peace spiritually and is balanced enough not to indulge in the excesses of Fire. All that pain, hard work, and intense searching has finally paid off, and it is others who will benefit most.

The Element of Air

Gemini   Libra   Aquarius

Fig. 8: The Air Signs

We now move back into a Masculine Element, so the whole environment changes. Like Fire, Air moves quickly forwards, outwards, or upwards, preferring height and light. These two Elements do complement each other by "facilitating" each other's actions. They allow, coax, and support the other. Fire (imagination) needs Air to communicate and articulate Fire's imaginative dreams and visions. Without Air's social graces and polite ways, Fire stampedes in all the wrong places. Air (ideas) needs Fire to warm and invigorate it, giving those ideas movement and passion. These are the two parts of the Masculine and together they are understandably formidable; although Air is looking for ideas and patterns to make sense, it wants to process and connect. That's far too much detail for Fire; Fire just "knows" without wanting to think about it, and gets impatient with Air.

Another psychological astrology dynamic—the Air Element is opposite to the Feminine Element of Water, a relationship we will cover more in the Water section.

So what are the basics of Air, and how are we to understand it best?

One of the most important concepts to grasp is that Air is about relating but it is not emotive, or motivated by emotions. The word "relate" has different meanings and the one we are studying here is in the context of "relates to." And "relates to" means applies to, coordinates with, refers to, with reference to, appertains to, or belongs with.

The opposite Element of Water does the slushy (forgive the pun!) emotional stuff and Air does the connecting, contacting, and communicating. It creates the clean, organized, socially attractive environment to meet in.

This rather detached Element separates things, allowing scrutiny because they are no longer bunched together. The air around us fills the space in between things, seemingly keeping them apart. Air is also a spatial Element, meaning it is about the space in between things. In our current understanding, it fills the spaces in this three-dimensional world. However, we also need to make room for the possibility that the Element of Air has rulership over any communication of an extraterrestrial or supernatural kind. Uranus and Aquarius in particular are equipped to "tune in" to Higher Mind vibrations of a multidimensional nature.

This is a difficult Element to grasp—literally. Thinking about their terrestrial equivalents, we can touch and feel water and earth. We can see and feel the heat of fire. We only know air is not there when we can't breathe; it is an invisible life support. We only know air is there when it moves, and actually Air signs do enjoy and partake of thinking that moves between one thing and another.

And that is a key to understanding the Air of astrology; it moves and connects up, it networks. The air of our atmosphere is a medium that allows flight and connection. It transmits sound waves and allows us to relate using words.

Air signs can be described as sociable, and social; they certainly seem friendly enough. They listen deeply and concernedly in conversations with others, but the truth is they are really harvesting new and different opinions to analyze and ponder over. They find people interesting (at the time!) and they want to know about them, so they strike up a dialogue and cross-question, in the nicest possible way.

They think about the morals, values, and principles of people and weigh up the pros and cons of their right or wrong behaviour by using the logical mind and not the gut. This means they tend not to leap quickly like Fire does—they dwell on things, they will think it through because they really appreciate a different, or new, point of view, idea, and opinion. This is what motivates them; they love it and eat it up with gusto.

They need space to do all this, so there is no cluttering of the mental processes. Hence, if they are angry with someone they may well sharply withdraw to allow the emotional storm to pass. This is not a moody withdrawal; they know they have to think themselves into a fairer-minded, objective appraisal of the other person's point of view. That can't happen in the middle of a heated argument. To consider all kinds of different opinions, they need to rationalize without any emotion, so they don't discriminate through anger in the heat of the moment. That would not be logical.

A really irritating trait is the need to play devil's advocate, in order to have a good debate. It then feels like they are taking the opposite corner, but they are really just trying to get under the skin of the other person, so they can look at all sides equally. It is all "brain gym" stuff. Anything for more brain fodder.

Air is the most separate Element, leading me to believe that our brains are the most separate part of us! Whoever designed us has not got it right yet.

Air thinks about consequences. Virgo does a little of that when it discriminates—yes to this bit, no to that bit—but Air truly analyzes and thinks, "If I do this, then that will be the consequence. This could happen if I put that wire there . . . but if I put it here, then that could happen."

Air encompasses culture and language, which names things and allows shared experience. Words record things in detail. But writing words down also separates intuition, instinct, and gut reaction (Fire) from the brain (Air).

Communication, trade, commerce, supply lines, and the exchange of things all come under Air. Strongly Air people match up need and surplus. This shop should sell that product. Or, this person needs that information, I must get it to them.

Human civilization suits Air because it values mental intelligence, and rewards it with academic success. Those people with a lot of Air signs highlighted in their birth chart read books and store knowledge; education suits them. Air truly thinks outside of the box, inventing, designing, and furthering consumerism. Psychology and astrology are a natural fit.

In normal social encounters Air people are gracious and likeable, with stimulating conversation and a tolerance for others' points of view. They value and give credit to any opinion, even if it is a world away from their own. However, the expression of feelings is generally enough to turn them right off.

People with a lot of Air in their birth charts usually remain cool and detached in response to displays of emotion. Tears and emotional begging can often get an upwards roll of the eyes. Reach into the dark shadow of the Air Element and you may find behaviour that is so distant, aloof, and detached from feeling and empathy that you start making comparisons to Spock on *Star Trek*.

Because they are not at ease in emotional waters, they have difficulty managing their own. If they are pitched into a huge emotional loss, they can "break down" because the mental circuit-breakers overload and blow. The results can be varied—from extreme reactions with lots of wailing and uncontrollable sobbing, to a freezing of emotional capacity and no outward sign that anything has happened at all.

Occasionally, because they cannot process emotions or find a way to live with them, the Air person will withdraw suddenly and completely with no explanation. They just cut off and "disappear." They enter a strange world of self-inflicted amnesia or self-isolation. Because this is the most "separate" Element, maybe that is the most comfortable thing to do. (Water does this too, but for reasons that are far more tragic.)

Having said all that, you may find it difficult to believe that the Air signs consider themselves good at the dynamics of human relating and often work in jobs where they promote cooperation, compromise, and harmony in social, workplace, or romantic relations. And funnily enough, they do well in such roles, because they are friendly and good communicators.

Also on the plus side, they often adjust and adapt with ease because they don't cling to anything. With no emotional baggage and old boyfriends tied to their ankles, making changes is easy to do. You want to grab two cheap tickets for a weekend in Rome? Air can usually accommodate such things.

Romantic relationships are their Achilles heel though, since partners usually want emotional responses when Air would rather detach and analyze instead. Without doubt, the biggest heartbreaks that I see are caused by people in love with prominent Air signs who cannot return the required emotional responses and just cut them off.

In spite of this, Air signs do want relationships, or they'd have nothing to analyze. It is just that they don't want the emotional, clingy bit. They like space, but they don't want to be on their own either. They are too social to like loneliness.

When Air does want close emotional contact, however, which does happen sometimes (there is Water in that birth chart somewhere), they have no idea how to ask for it and usually go all around the houses, sometimes unable to show the desire openly. Then they get huffy when the partner didn't seem to recognize the signals by osmosis and oblige by making the overtures. The partner is usually too frightened to make the overtures, since they are nearly always rebuffed!

The symbol for Gemini is a set of twins. The symbol for Libra is a set of balance scales, originally with a child god in a Sun disc on top of the fulcrum, or below it. The symbol for Aquarius is the Ancient Egyptian deity Hapi, who holds an amphora vase in each hand, from which something "watery" is pouring. Hapi is the god of the flooding of the River Nile with life-giving water. He is also connected to something the Egyptians called magical, healing, or sweet water, which purified two *udjat* eyes representing the Sun and full Moon. There are no animals in these symbols, only human-style deity figures. Whether by accident or design, this is a convenient reminder of how different the Air signs are. Note the "two" theme? A set of twins, a set of balancing scales with two sides, and a deity holding two amphoras to tend two *udjat* eyes. The theme of two is symbolic of balance and Ma'at. Maybe the ancient Egyptians found duality or polarity particularly meaningful.

~ GEMINI ~
Air Zodiac Sign

Glyph Ⅱ
Third Sign of the Zodiac Belt
Lowest Air Sign
"I think"
Ruled by Mercury
Symbol is the Twins

This chapter does not refer to Gemini as a Sun sign but to the Gemini energy that exists in all of us to a degree. Geminis or the Gemini types discussed here simply have more of it than most.

Decades ago, one of my astrology teachers said that the Gemini energy was like a meatball with arms. My Sun in Gemini was quite insulted at the time, but I have come to understand this insight completely. It is the superficiality and lack of depth that makes Gemini so notable. It doesn't offer up any resistance—it just goes along with things. It follows, morphs, adapts, changes, and facilitates other, stronger energies and drives. Gemini Sun signs may not be so lightweight, but that is because the Sun is no pushover and they have other planets and zodiac signs in their charts that will compensate and assert strength.

Gemini is the zodiac sign for communication and I think it is important to make the point that this is a "service" that allows ideas and information to be passed on. Hence it may be useful that it is such a whimsical energy because it has a low impact on content; it simply passes material on.

So, Geminian people like connecting people up so they can "pass things on." Ann Smith says she is looking for a bicycle, so when Gemini energy hears that Joe Bloggs is selling one, it will put one in touch with the other. Jane at work's cat has just had a litter of kittens and Mrs Brown's cat has died—maybe she would like to know how to get another one?

They also take pleasure in comparing and contrasting this with that. Left to their own devices, a Geminian person will visit one supermarket and make a note of the range and the prices, then visit the store over the road and compare prices. This may not be because of financial pressures; they just like doing it. They enjoy movement and discovering the world around them, so a trip from one supermarket to another is a joy.

Having said that, Geminian types are wheelers and dealers and they do enjoy snapping up a bargain. Not for the money—that doesn't matter as much to them—it is the thrill of exploiting the system of promotional items. Or being in the right place at the right time to get that last, heavily discounted frying pan.

Bargaining, bartering, and negotiating a big purchase is like manna from heaven to them. They love it when they close a lucrative deal; it proves how clever they are, and they love being clever and witty. They also like working in sales, nattering away to the customers, and keeping an eye out for an opportunity to pass on information. Equally, they want to hear about new experiences and the ideas that others have. They can add this to the vast amount of information already stored in their memory banks.

Geminians go in for lots of variety but rarely take any deeper meaning from it. They like to talk for pleasure and their conversations go all over the place as they jump from one subject to another. The Gemini mind is like the mental version of a kaleidoscope as it changes shape; just as you are admiring one shape, it changes to another and you have to start again. They take mischievous delight in running rings around slower minds with their lightning-fast mental processes.

The trouble with this is that their opinions change daily. No idea is fixed, it's all fluid and changeable. The Gemini energy transforms constantly, like changing cloud patterns in the sky. In fact, if you watch a weather report, they will show you a computer-simulated, fast-moving video of cloud formations as they flit across the surface of the Earth. Never remaining in one place, forever taking up a new position, and experiencing a different perspective. So it is, in the world of Gemini energy.

And this does indeed produce "debateable" results. In the mind of someone with a lot of Gemini energy, a strong, determined statement is a starting point, not a finishing line, so it should be debated, and is open to adjustment or replacement. This works both ways, so the Geminian can be given a hard and fast rule and immediately want to challenge it with questions and logical alternatives. Or the Geminian can make a clear, unequivocal statement, but then not stick to it themselves.

They are always open to being persuaded into a different opinion. This could be seen as flexibility or fickleness, and quite annoying to more reliable creatures. Perhaps all butterflies have a Gemini Sun sign? The two species have a lot in common.

Just as annoying might be the need to see both sides of the argument. They will play devil's advocate just to see what can be learned of the other side. "What happens if I ask this question, or pose that point of view?" Understandably, they might be accused of disloyalty when they appear to condone the other side.

This goes as far as wondering what a serial murderer was thinking of. Or asking a man why he beats his wife. The curiosity doesn't stop at the dark side. The god associated with Gemini is Hermes, the only god allowed into and out of the Underworld. There doesn't seem to be anywhere the Gemini mind won't go.

All this makes Geminians appear unprincipled, undiplomatic, or lacking in emotional sensitivity. But on the other hand, they make great journalists and academic students, because they always want to see the other side too.

Going back to Hermes, he was also the god of thieves, and in the dark side of Geminian energy is how good they are at being crooks, villains, and deceitful con men. But Geminians do not go out looking for a fight; in fact they are definite cowards. Physical violence is not their thing. They much prefer a good stimulating debate. The pain of violent attack appals them. Gemini happily sidesteps violence, leaving that to Fire signs and Scorpio. Maybe they just cannot become so committed to one opinion that they are prepared to fight for it.

Their innocent curiosity gets them into a lot of tight corners and, sooner or later, they will get the blame for everything. As they don't go in for physical violence, it can be difficult to defend themselves, but if they can get a way to talk themselves out of trouble then they are safe. Early education can be problematic because they easily get bored and restless, but if they get a good teacher who makes things interesting, then they are usually quick to learn. They lack the ability to concentrate and need someone to sit and discuss things with. If they have someone to keep them on track and focussed, it makes all the difference to producing homework or getting captivated by something else.

It goes without saying that they all have a book in there somewhere. They love stories and are clever with words, so it is a shame if they can't point to something that got published, even if it is just an article somewhere online. They can write very clever, sophisticated, and effective letters to complain about something, or put a point of view forward, so maybe "Letters to the Editor" would be a good place to start.

But . . . for all they relish decimating the providers of poor service, they have great difficulty writing personal letters. This comes from their aversion to describing and experiencing private feelings. It is so much easier to point out that the traffic problems at the local shopping centre would be considerably reduced if they introduced a one-way system. That would be logical.

Personal messages? Phew! What if your words were interpreted incorrectly? If feelings don't feel comfortable, why and how do you attempt to describe them? Geminians dislike writing about their own feelings. It is okay to read about somebody else's, that is simply part of their curiosity about others. But their own? Yuk!

Now—books! Geminians will tell you they love books, and certainly they all have a pile of books. But note the bookmarks halfway through them! They will pick out the best bits and leave the rest of the book unread.

The same could be said of relating and relationships too. If only they could pick out the best bits and leave the rest with a bookmark halfway through! Firstly, a partner needs to be continuously interesting, and that is a tall order. They have to be a good conversationalist above all else. If the Gemini mind is not entertained, then a George Clooney lookalike would not be enough to make that relationship last. Geminians get impatient with domesticity and boring people, and relating might include both. But since they like having fun and flirting, and depending on other parts of the chart, they can engage in triangles, and that keeps life interesting.

The best way to keep a Gemini romance going is to keep up a good social life with lots of stimulating friends and a variety of entertainment.

They can and do fall in love, but it has to be with a best friend and an intelligent communicator. They are not particularly interested in being with a famous or wealthy person, but they really, really don't want anyone clipping their wings and hanging emotional blackmail around them.

As for the dark side . . .

Let me see . . . fickle, non-committal—some astrologers talk about mood swings, with lots of different faces. However, I don't know if that is a result of all the other, stronger, zodiac signs taking control now and then. Gemini is quite weak as an energy. It is possible that extreme amounts of Gemini will result in attention deficit hyperactivity disorder.

They usually suffer from insomnia—not occasionally, usually. Their brains just don't stop and it keeps them awake. And they can struggle with emotional breakdown or health problems if too bored or confined.

~ LIBRA ~

Air Zodiac Sign

Glyph ♎

Seventh Sign of the Zodiac Belt
Middle Air Sign
"I balance"
Ruled by Juno and Venus
Symbol is the Balance Scales

This chapter does not refer to Libra as a Sun sign but to the Libran energy that exists in all of us to a degree. Librans or the Libra types discussed here simply have more of it than most.

Let's get to the heart of something right away. On the surface the energy of Libra is courteous, amiable, friendly, and gracious. But scratch the surface and the innocent sweetness soon disappears. Librans are no Barbie dolls, despite what astrology websites and perhaps even Libra itself will tell you. There are two sides to this energy and, granted, one is diplomatic, gracious, attractive—but also intellectual, civilized, fair, and polite. The *other* side is indecisive, cold, quarrelsome, demanding, combative, and controlling.

It is true that Libra energy aspires to a beautiful and harmonious environment, with colour coordination and flowers, but Libra backs this up with Air's perceptive intelligence and strategic intellectualism. This is a Masculine sign and don't you forget it. Otherwise, you will get quite a shock when you catch a glimpse of the opposite sign of Aries breaking through the self-contained Libran Air, and firing a few missiles. Remember, each sign contains the seeds of its opposite sign on the zodiac wheel. Libra contains the seeds of Aries, and, when sufficiently off balance, Masculine energy surges outward.

It is all to do with those scales, which are a mechanical object after all. The Libran nature is devoted to the mechanics of balancing them, and so strives to be fair and equal. Note, I am talking about the Libra version of fair and equal here. We all have our own version. Libra is credited with a strong sense of justice, but we are talking the Air version of justice. This fight will go as far as "an eye for an eye, and a tooth for a tooth." Libra and the opposite sign of Aries share an opposition of conflict, no matter how gracious Libra people seem to be.

Even under normal circumstances they will expect a fair exchange. Libran thinking runs along the lines of "If I do this for you, then I expect that in return. I bought you some shopping on my way here, so you should clean my car out in exchange." Libra energy will pay its own way and stress over dividing the restaurant bill exactly in half because that is the correct thing to do.

There is a particular behaviour that all strongly Libran people unconsciously adopt: If they are trying to decide something they will seek everyone else's opinion. They will phone friends. Turn to a complete stranger in a shop and ask them. The whole yoga class, everyone at the school gate . . . But what then? Do they they make lists and add up all the "no's" and "yes's?" Well . . . no. They don't. Can you believe it, they don't want anyone else to make their mind up for them, so they just do what they want to do! Seriously. They have been fair and asked around, briefly weighed up all the answers, but then thrown a few weights of their own on their favoured end.

Something we will learn more about later is that Libra is a "cardinal" energy, which means it has to instigate and initiate independently of outside opinion. So, they will always ask everybody else's opinions . . . but then make their own mind up, without taking any of those opinions into account. Amazing. They just needed to bat against another, because their world is dual, not singular. Here's a little trick to get them to make a decision: The Libran will quickly make their mind up if you try to do it for them. A snap decision will appear. Here is an example. You have been waiting as patiently as the McDonald's team member for them to place their food order. Big Mac or quarter pounder . . . Big Mac or . . . a chicken salad . . . Say in a firm voice, "I'll decide for you—the Big Mac!" Immediately the Libran will make a decision. "No! The Filet-o-Fish!" Don't believe me? Try it.

This is where their need for a dual world collides with their own authority to initiate or instigate. Let's look at this further.

There is a little-known secret to understanding the psychology of the Libran nature and it is built into their conception of the perfect relationship: the World of Two. Where two people or two things are the right balance. Like two candlesticks on the mantlepiece standing at each end, in perfect symmetry. So firstly, there has to be a significant other, and then they will idealize this lover because, together, they are raised into that World of Two.

Unfortunately, Libran energy wants the honeymoon rose-tinted glasses to last for ever, so they are devastated when this idyllic person has dirty feet and bad breath.

Librans put an enormous amount of time and energy into relationships. They are masters of attention and flattery to start with—but watch out. When romantic love turns into basic human relating, which it must do eventually, Libra usually takes off the rose-tinted spectacles and starts being critical. The relationship isn't turning out to be perfect.

If the very relationship is threatened, Libra will become unbalanced. Since two is the magic number, the company of the Other is the most crucial need. Hence fairness now has to take second place, and Libra will give way to keep the relationship. But . . . the Libran scales are now out of balance, and things will become more and more difficult for them. Living with an unequal relationship puts them into defence mode and they will emotionally cut off (Air sign) even while still being physically present. Sex will be the first thing to go, since they can at least control access to their bodies. Libra energy flips, becoming critical, spiteful, and volatile.

Few partners will remain past this point. (For various reasons, Cancerians, Capricorns, and Pisceans are the exception.) Eventually, even the Libran person becomes disillusioned and "falls out of love." They themselves must match up to their own sense of perfection, and they disappoint themselves when they don't. They will recognize that they don't like what they have become.

This brings on the guilt, and invokes hatred of the relationship, which brings on more scenes of anger. Libra will usually end the relationship at this stage—or the fear of NOT being in a relationship might be so great that Libra may *still* hang on.

Here is the problem for Libras: if you are always preaching the holier-than-thou answer to the Perfect Relationship and have a certificate in counselling to prove you are superior in this, then you look and feel pretty silly when you can't stop being jealous and secretly prying into your partner's phone. Being an Air sign with a need for space, Libra really does not want to be seen as a jealous, grasping wife. Unstable Libran emotions are painful and distressing for everyone involved. But their downfall comes from an inability to discuss their own emotions. If they could honestly explain and express their secret fears and insecurities, they might find a willing listener to sympathize and understand. They need to learn how to ask for help when they feel their relating "expertise" is failing them, and help with how to approach their partner with humility and love over not getting it right or failing to understand. They need to learn how to hold their hand out for a hug, something that Water finds so easy.

So . . . here we have the Sign of relating and yet it seems the people with the most Libran energy have the most difficult time. The Air Element imbues them with a need for space, a dislike of emotional closeness, a picky perfection gene, and ideals that are impossible to achieve in a human relationship. Libra is the middle sign of the Air zodiac signs and, as such, is the most painful. There are so many relationship conflicts to recognize, process, work through, and try to perfect, while Libra types lack unconditional amounts of tolerance, forgiveness, and acceptance of basic human fumbling.

Thinking comes with the territory for the Air signs and Libra energy is no exception. Libra types will try to consider every point of view. So much so that they can fail to make decisions as they get wrapped up in rethinking, reassessing, re-perfecting. They want to be fair-minded and don't want to miss a single point of view or another angle. They want to be seen to be doing the right thing, so they check and correct their thinking over and over again. This may not serve the gods of fairness, however, since anybody doing this will generally re-colour events to give themselves a more favourable position.

Maybe, in reality, Librans generally don't like other people (there is always a point in their lives when they are actually scared of people), but they are not able to be this honest, either with themselves or with others. People aren't perfect, but still Librans are born to believe they can perfect them, have an input, and make a difference.

And this is the sign of human relating . . . why? I've thought about this often and I think there is a little-known, esoteric reason, which I will run past you.

We are born into this dimension with a birth chart describing our own particular set of struggles. Difficult conflicts that we are destined to live out over our lives. Why? We are doing this on behalf of the cosmos. In this way, the cosmos is learning and refining itself as time goes on because our experience and learning is fed back to the invisible, spiritual world. All the internal conflicts of the cosmos get to be worked on and answers are found and improvements made. When we die, our knowledge and wisdom is absorbed by the invisible World Soul Lake and this improves the quality of it for the next takers. Hence, none of our struggle is wasted and our contribution has value; as with all the zodiac signs, Libra's task isn't supposed to be easy—it has a spiritual purpose.

This energy can be diplomatic enough to agree with one side of a dispute, and then agree with the other side too because they just don't like falling out with people. Their thinking is that if they fall out with people too often, there will be no one to balance things with. Hence, they are prone to trying to keep everyone in harmonious energy.

They like to initiate diplomatic talks and actions towards better, more ideal relationships. But they want to lead others carefully and diplomatically. So they choose words carefully, like "we" to indicate partnership and "working together."

Many Libran-type people are sensitive to being disliked, which makes them uncomfortably aware of the disapproval of others. There is a real irony to this because on the one hand they seek approval, and on the other they want to chastise and "perfect" the relating skills of others, which earns them the criticism they can't stand. They often think about these kinds of dilemmas, which causes consternation and then makes them difficult to relate to!

Because Librans need other people to balance and be friends with, they like to appeal to others. They are susceptible to flattery and attention themselves and they know how to give it to create a harmonious and engaging exchange. This is when they are at their most gracious and appealing.

Which leads us to their great gifts in life. Design and styling, whether it is interior, exterior, grand scale, or a windowsill. This is where they excel. The ideals of symmetry and perfection, harmony and balance are executed with expertise, even if they have never had formal training. This Sun sign is naturally attuned to the clever and delightful use of colour and space with any materials. They organize what is to hand beautifully. An old ribbon from Christmas, vintage embroidered doilies from the linen cupboard, and a plant with the right coloured pot magically appear and make the old window ledge look so pretty.

Or perhaps a scented candle and the quiet removal of the source of an offending smell. Give them an hour in a room crying out for attention and you won't recognize it afterwards. Librans can introduce grace, balance, and style to a tent in the Egyptian desert or a messy bachelor pad. How about a tray of food for an invalid? See how the coral-coloured napkins match the colour of the poached salmon in scallop shells? This is where Libran people excel. You will find them in garden centres, carefully turning the pots round so the flowers are showing their best. Maybe a florist's shop, where their uncanny knack for arranging flowers makes them the best in the area. Garden design, interior design . . . you get the idea.

Another fitting career would be one in clothing, either designing or retailing. You can imagine their window-dressing skills. This also goes for graphic design and website-building. When Libran energy is in the right environment, designing or dressing something, they can be so utterly charming, friendly, and gracious, you wouldn't guess they had a single issue with anything. And they don't, actually. It is the watery world of human emotions that unseats them.

They find it so hard to articulate their emotions because they are embarrassing and illogical and make no sense, so really they would prefer it if you guessed what they want, rather than have to spell it out. This is generally where it all starts to go so horribly wrong.

Perhaps if Librans could dial down the criticisms of imperfections, their own as well as everyone else's, and introduce humour as a diversion, relationship life might be less challenging. Laughing at yourself with a partner is usually the best relationship healer there is.

~ AQUARIUS ~
Air Zodiac Sign

Glyph 〰〰

Eleventh Sign of the Zodiac Belt
Highest Air Sign
"I rebel"
Ruled by Uranus

This chapter does not refer to Aquarius as a Sun sign but to the Aquarius energy that exists in all of us to a degree. Aquarians or the Aquarius types discussed here simply have more of it than most.

Symbol is the Water Bearer. See the end of this section for a discussion on this.

Aquarian-type people are here for everyone, and belong to no one. They don't like people, but they love their friends. And what they really, truly want in a romantic relationship is . . . freedom. So, the more they love, the less they want you around. Sound a bit weird? Well, they are. And more than that, they pride themselves on weirdness. Cranky, different, way-out, fringe individuals appeal to them and they dislike formal, mainstream social climbers. To be able to keep that kind of standpoint in a world that is built around status and money requires stubbornness, and that they have by the bucketload.

The funny thing is, they can see clearly how everyone else and the world ought to change, and they will pontificate on that—however, they are strangely "fixed" and resistant to change themselves. Which—of course—they won't admit!

Imagine being born a mutinous rebel, but also stubbornly resistant to change. You'd have to be pretty determined not to hear the criticism, right? Well, that is when it is handy to be dogmatic and really indifferent to the opinions of others. Aquarian-type people can manage that. They can be really cut off from anything others think. Handy if you are a scientist who wants to prove the rest of the community wrong.

Let's take a journey out into the solar system for a few minutes, because there we will find some interesting synchronicity between the energy of Aquarius and the planet that rules it.

Uranus is unusual. Well, more than unusual. Downright impossible actually. The mechanics of the solar system means that, generally, all of the planets have a north and south pole that align in the same direction, much the same as the Earth. Let's say their poles go from top to bottom and they spin round this axis. Uranus does not do this; it is the only planet that lies on its side, compared to the others. Its north and south poles are on a plane with our equator. No one can fully explain this and it doesn't make sense. Does that not talk of rebellion and a need to be different? And indeed, being different is something Aquarius types take great pride in.

Remember Leo? The Fire sign with a strong need to be different, unique, and special. Well, Leo is the opposite sign to Aquarius and together these two signs form an opposition that, first of all, seeks to reveal and revere the divine spirit, ego, pride, or Fire within us (the Leo end).

Aquarius takes that confident Leo Fire into a bigger arena where it will have to hold its own. So the Aquarian energy warns that we are not special, we are just one single ant in the ant colony, or one grain of sand on the beach.

You are probably starting to get the correct impression—Aquarius energy and Aquarians are different. They are eccentric, visionary, rebellious, stubborn, and free-spirited, with access to higher intelligence. Their skills are far removed from romantic relationships and the emotionalism that is so inherently human.

Hidden in there somewhere, even if the individual does not access this, are the most far-reaching and advanced ideas for the human race. This energy embraces mathematics and advanced sciences, such as quantum physics or astrophysics, but they may be hesitant to put these ideas forward because they genuinely don't want to get into the limelight. Then some other "idiot" (their words) puts their views into the public arena and Aquarius will finally stand up and argue it, maybe being outspoken, tactless, and brusque while they are at it.

Aquarius is outspoken and doesn't care, but they pride themselves on being big respecters of the truth. (Their version!) Aquarius energy can easily shock or startle, while they would prefer to think that they are helping others awaken from the induced slumber of the masses.

So, how does your average Aquarian-type person live in this world? The need for larger groups than the family is a huge influence, so this energy will be found in communes or group-living situations more than any other. The free love movement is or was Aquarian in nature, and where you find agreements on polyamory (multiple sexually relating partners), you will find an Aquarian or a Piscean.

Why? Because the Aquarian energy works in bigger and wider concepts than just a single partner. Unless they have a packed working and social life too, one is just not enough and potentially boring. Admittedly, as they get older it is usually a career that they give all their time to, because it contains so much more potential for the new and exciting. I think it was Linda Goodman who wrote in the 1970s that this is the sign least likely to marry or have a relationship.

Liberation and freedom are big ideals. But freedom from what? It is pretty hard to get freedom from everything, so leaving aside that option—anything else really.

Aquarius comes after Capricorn on the zodiac wheel and it is as if the rebel Aquarian energy has to break down the Capricorn formality and materialism, with all those rules and restraints. Earth signs might want everything set into concrete, but Air wants freedom.

Aquarian-type people prefer to join with a group of other "enlightened thinkers" to challenge and bring down the elite. But they rarely make solitary attempts. This is so they don't stick out from the crowd as Leo would be happy to do.

Leo is born to find the specialness within, to grow to love their inner child and ego: to believe they are special. Aquarius energy says no ego is special, and they really dislike making anyone feel special or different. Individual choice is irrelevant, cosmic truth is all. So they can be very impatient with ego-centred people.

Some more quirkiness: Aquarian-type people can have a really engaged conversation with you one day, but walk straight by you the next. A little later you may see them in an animated 30-minute conversation with the postman, enquiring about his colleagues and the postal strike. Then the next day they will ignore him. Perhaps the postman is just another ant in the colony, while his part in the rebellion was very interesting!

What about the factory worker who is happy to see his workmates every day, but no longer has any engagement with his wife, who he still lives with while knowing nothing about her? He probably does not connect emotionally to anyone, likes going to a football game on a Saturday for its group euphoria and camaraderie, but otherwise is brusque, insensitive, and unfeeling. His wife gave up trying to talk to him long ago and spends her time with neighbours or the grandchildren. Perhaps her dad was the same, so she sees no need to rock the boat; this is "normal."

On the other hand, we might get a humanitarian thinker who has high ideals for the welfare of the group. His principles and ethics lead him to become a local politician, social worker, or some other occupation where he can join a group dealing with social issues. Groups don't make emotional demands of individuals and Aquarian-type males are very uncomfortable with their own feelings, and scared to death of anybody else's. So a group is safe.

Ex-partners of Aquarian-type men often bemoan that he wants to be "friends" after they have broken up; actually that is quite a compliment, because they value friends. Unfortunately, anyone unlucky enough to be in a romantic relationship with an Aquarian-type man has to live with the fact that they will never feel special to them and their man needs a lot of space and free time. Fine if you are both international air crew.

Aquarian-type females also prefer logic to emotions and want a friend for a mate, but they are not so attachment-phobic as males. They tend to focus on the home and apply their very high ideals to the cleaning and decorating. The Aquarian need for straight lines and uncluttered surfaces is usually evident, and out of choice their home would be full of easily cleaned glass and stainless steel. A few have such an acute nervous system that it can lead to an apparent nervous tic and obsessive behaviour around house cleaning. Their high standards should also go down well at work. They are often drawn to psychiatry and psychology because these are, after all, logical.

Although Aquarians can count more than their fair share of geniuses in their midst, they are not skilled in debate or argument like Gemini. They get lost in the pros and cons because their minds aren't flexible enough to shift positions quickly. They can be "singular" and "fixed" thinkers in simple human exchange. Because of this fixity, they won't budge an inch, no matter how convincingly you have put your argument. However, this fixed thinking is good for rigorously pursuing "fringe" beliefs or out-of-this-world concepts. Whether it is Covid denial, UFOs or the second coming of a messiah, they won't be put off their stance.

Their other weakness is avoiding all emotional context. So, in mentally discarding all the emotional content of an argument, they can lose their point. If the evidence against them is overwhelming, they'll just leave, simply cut out. Their best defence is to disappear.

I read years ago that Aquarians dislike mainstream education, so many home-school their children. Thinking this sounded a little over the top, it actually is more prevalent than I would have thought.

Let's look at the zodiac signs in a different way, like the layers of an onion. So Aries is in the centre and Taurus is the next layer out. Then comes Gemini, followed by Cancer, and so on. All the way out to the eleventh layer, where Aquarius lies. Now the onion's skin is more papery, tougher, and getting browner. Conditions on the outside of that onion are very different from the ones in the middle where it is moist and protected.

What is in that "outer world?" There is no doubt all kinds of life, consciousness, spookiness, and even different deities out there; we just haven't discovered any of this yet. Recently identified planets far out into space confirm that, in time, humans will leave Earth.

It is the Aquarius energy in humans that will make contact with alien entities. This questing archetype, found in all humans but most especially those who are attracted by the space industry, will lead the way. Science fiction movies that explore beyond the solar system and take us into strange new galaxies attract Aquarian-style actors. For example, Richard Dean Anderson, who plays Jack O'Neill in *Stargate SG1*, has a big chunk of Aquarius in his birth chart.

If there is any doubt about the alien talents of our friendly Aquarian types, then think about this one. They can be talking on the phone while listening to the weather report and they will still hear the conversation at the other end of the room. They can take in and comprehend many audio channels at once.

Let us turn to the out-of-this-world, cosmic aspect of Aquarius. Our universe is an organized dimension in the cosmos of many dimensions. Possibly there are higher planes of existence and one or more of these could be occupied by the Element of Air in a form that is unknown to us at this time. However, we are sure that Uranus (ruler of Aquarius) and Aquarius resonate with electricity, plasma, electromagnetic forces, and wave communication. Since all of these are found in brains, maybe there is a macro universal mind with similar behaviour out there somewhere. If there is, Aquarius and Uranus are our links to it.

In recent years I have come to develop my opinion of Air's extraordinary potential, and I now see that the futuristic, Aquarian side of this strange Element has yet to be understood. In fact, it is only just dimly coming into view on the horizon of our existence. It is likely that only science will eventually give us a full understanding of Air.

We probably had a better grasp of it around the fifth century BCE when the Greek Derveni papyrus was written. In it, we are told that "air/Mind" never came to be—it existed before anything else, and will always be. Go back to page 13, "The Psychology of Masculine and Feminine Behaviour," and you will read that the same was said of the Feminine. Maybe they both existed before anything else? There are several important ancient texts that support the theory of a higher mind that *thought* our dimension into existence *from* its outer plane of existence.

Probably, Air will become clearer in the future when Uranus moves through Gemini from 2025 to 2033 while Pluto is still in Aquarius. Aquarius is the sign of astrology and Pluto changes the characteristics of the sign it is moving through. During this time, support for Western religions may decline more quickly than ever and science and astrology may undergo a period of stupendous breakthroughs. Artificial intelligence will grow in influence and the chances of talking to aliens get closer. New knowledge, higher awareness, and fantastic new forms of communication and A.I. could all merge into the predicted Dawning of Aquarius—a planetary-wide change in the tidal forces of human consciousness and ideals.

And now we turn to the symbol for Aquarius, which is controversial. (Well, why wouldn't it be?) The oldest one we know of comes from the Dendera Temple in Egypt. It is often interpreted as a man pouring water and he is even called "the water bearer." Over time, this has become a number of things, one of which is the image of a man down on one knee, balancing a vessel on his shoulder that is open at both ends. Some say this signifies our human capacity for serving as both a container and channel for universal consciousness.

But how could this be? Aquarius is not a Water sign. Could the astrologers of the day have been muddled? In Ancient Egypt, the figure is actually the androgynous Egyptian deity Hapi, the god of the River Nile's yearly flooding. Without this precious inundation, the Egyptians would not have been able to farm, feed themselves, or travel easily. They fully recognised the spiritual importance of this holy event and much of their religious activity was devoted to it. The dual aspects of masculine and feminine in this one deity was probably in recognition of both fertility and growth.

The hieroglyph for water is a zigzag line and Hapi pours a zigzag line from each of two flasks. However, the Egyptian symbol for water occasionally infers the use of sacred, magical, healing, sweet, life-giving "pure" water, reserved for the most holy ceremonies, including the baptism or coronation of the pharaoh. In which case, the contents could best be described as a higher sacred "life force," watery or otherwise.

The Element of Water

Cancer   Scorpio   Pisces

Fig. 9: The Water Signs

"Of all the elements, the Sage should take Water as his preceptor. Water is yielding but all-conquering. Water extinguishes Fire or, finding itself likely to be defeated, escapes as steam and reforms. Water washes away soft Earth or, when confronted by rocks, seeks a way around . . . It saturates the atmosphere so that wind (Air) dies. Water gives way to obstacles with deceptive humility, for no power can prevent it following its destined course to the sea. Water conquers by yielding; it never attacks but always wins the last battle." An eleventh-century Chinese scholar.

The Element of Water represents our emotions, sensitivities, and feelings of love. It also represents memories and the past. And the past can mean even the primal terror, creation, and our earliest human evolution. We are in the Feminine polarity once more, so Water draws in and clings, it heals, it is instinctive rather than verbal, it is pervasive and seeps rather than being aggressive or combative.

Water holds the seeds of life; or, at least, our creation myths tell us that all life springs from water. It connects us to all life and evolution. Water is a medium of our world and the invisible realm of dark matter and energy that flows all around us unseen and unfelt. It flows, connects, and mediates throughout Earthly and spiritual existence.

In the same way that human eggs and semen carry genetic code, spiritual Water has a mysterious "memory" that carries information about the past and origins. With the Watery energies in our birth charts we also feel the love and desire that fuel an unconscious and compulsive primal need to relate, copulate, and reproduce. The emotions involved in the selection of sexual partners, relationships, and in parent/child bonds are all held in this mysterious element. And as if

94

that isn't enough, the Water in the matriarchal line carries the family karma.

To explain this further: the female sex plays a mysterious role that is held within the Element of Water. It is a genetically carried, life-selecting role. An unconscious sexual selection process that has intelligence and memory and is played out through the generations of the matriarchal line.

It used to be thought that once fertilization has occurred, each sex makes an equal genetic contribution to the offspring. But science is beginning to say otherwise; there is research suggesting that female animals have much more "say," through the way they behave during pregnancy, in key traits like body size, cognitive ability, and personality. These traits might be formed by epigenetic inheritance, and the mother's DNA could actually protect her own epigenetic process while stripping out the father's.

In this way, in astrology, the soul/Watery traits and memories of lineage are reproduced through the generations. Most surprising is the way in which actual experiences re-occur. A report notes that if a child's grandparent experienced a famine, that influences the child's response to famine.

So perhaps in every generation a child is born to unmarried parents; or forced sex and domestic violence may reappear. If these issues are not dealt with, they snowball in the family matriarchal line until a special child is born who has so much karma or epigenetic family material gathered up, their life *has* to take on the family myth or skeletons in the cupboard and stop them happening again. Is this how the Cosmic Soul Lake learns and grows?

The invisible, epigenetic inheritance is revealed in the natal chart through the conditions surrounding Water zodiac signs, Water planets and most especially Water houses.

As if that wasn't enough, Water also strongly connects us with our own past experience of nurturing. Because Water is associated with unconscious habitual response patterns, it is the part of us that has most to do with unconscious reactions. Again, the spiritual element of Water stores memories from the past, but in this case it assimilates them into automatic responses, so that the human doesn't have to think about them again. It is then not necessary to spend conscious effort on formulating a response; it will just come naturally from these past memories. For instance, we "remember" loving and kissing and hugging from baby- or childhood, and do it automatically. We don't need to think about how to kiss and hug, it is an instinctive thing that just happens when we feel the right emotions.

Water processes emotional feelings. Because humans are built with a chemical system that feels, those with no access to Water in their birth charts still have emotions, but their emotions will operate outside their control and they will not be comfortable with them. In this case, their emotions, which are independent, powerful, and primal, could overwhelm them.

Pain, love, healing, and compassion are all carried in Water, so without this Element we would be fairly robotic. The Water in humans seems to draw pain towards itself; it metaphorically opens its arms and pulls the wounds and hurt towards itself. I think this is an unconscious reaction, and it has some side effects. Watery people cannot stop this from happening, so they will sense the pain of others and are extremely sensitive to atmospheres, which they read with their emotional barometer. Information comes from "feeling," not "thinking." They also absorb the emotions and feelings behind what is being said, rather than the words. It is then difficult to verbalize when someone is demanding a spoken explanation. Liking and disliking based on unexplained feelings can be annoying to non-watery partners.

Because they can't really control the mechanism that draws pain and need towards them, and because of their resulting involuntary empathy, Watery people will offer help and solace to anyone who needs it. This can also get them into trouble, because it looks like disloyalty; if your best friend's boyfriend is looking for somewhere to live because she threw him out, it is probably not wise to offer him your spare room!

Those with heavy emphasis on Water often have difficulty in gaining detachment or perspective because the feelings just overwhelm them. Hence they can never visit an animal shelter for fear of having to adopt—or they do visit and now have six cats.

This is a Feminine energy and picks up the ultra-soft end of the continuum, where individuals get used and abused. Certainly, Cancer and Pisces can be too submissive, too dependent, and too passive. (Earth sign Capricorn can make that claim too, but for the reason that it wants to toughen up by taking the hard road, which is a different motivation.)

While we are on the psychology of Water, I want to point out that water (and Water) clings. Watch the condensation on the outside of a drinking glass slide down and cling to the bottom, such is its cohesive nature. The properties of any of the Elements on our physical, earthly plane should always be examined for psychological information about the spiritual planes.

I have already said that pain draws Water towards it, but actually it is more than that. It works *both* ways, because they are symbiotic, or have a close mutual association. Moreover, grief, pain, and love are all on the psychological continuum of the Water Element. It is worth repeating the words of the late Queen Elizabeth II: "Grief is the price we pay for love." Grief and pain are at one end of the continuum, and love is at the other. Water features the broad range of "feeling."

So, Water bathes and heals and, probably, ancient healing systems like reiki use the spiritual Water of the invisible quantum realm. This mysterious Element, which transcends time and dimensions, has an emotional intelligence, but no reasoning powers. This is most obvious in the relating game, where emotions come with the territory. Let's take a scenario.

Air and Water are a couple at a party. Air socialises, connects, and chats while Water stands by the door and looks a little lost and out of it. So eventually Air walks over and wants to know what the problem is. As we have noted, Water is non-verbal and will feel hopelessly unable to explain its feelings. When nothing is forthcoming, Air loses patience and starts, between gritted teeth, to demand "better behaviour." Feeling miserable, Water moans, "You don't understand me—you're so cold." And Air replies, "You won't talk to me, but you expect me to understand you! You are not logical." They experience and react to the environment in fundamentally different ways, but also have different way of expressing themselves. Remember though, no one is born with only Air or only Water in their birth charts, so it is the "weight" of one over the other that modifies this possible scenario. This example is given to help us understand their differences as "opposite" Elements.

Let's look at some of the other issues that might arise with Watery people in relationships.

They can be overly loving or giving in a relationship, which can make the recipient uncomfortable with guilt at not reciprocating. Or it can result in the recipient becoming more and more abusive and eventually just too powerful for a meaningful or healthy relationship. However, if Watery people can find needy ones to support, then they can gain control by making the other feel so indebted. Water loves to feel needed and hates to feel rejected, so that works.

Speaking of which, there is a general fear of aloneness and of not relating. They need constant contact with people and a constant stream of Water/feeling flowing past them. Love and relationship give them security. Flowing tides of emotion don't distress them; in fact, tears are made of water, so they find their natural home here.

Water signs in general have few defences. They don't have Air's sarcastic tongue or Fire's immediate temper. What they tend to do is manipulate the atmosphere with moods or produce the emotional blackmail card.

Fire and Water have a good working relationship, but then Fire is resonant with the dark energy and Water is resonant with the dark matter of the quantum realm, where they also exist as the Masculine and Feminine polarities. Water can absorb a lot of Fire's excessive heat, and Fire can heat Water and get it on the move. In humans, Water can modify Fire's insensitive, dismissive actions, while Fire can instil joy and optimism in Water's moody pessimism.

If spiritual Fire is attention, faith, and belief, then we can say that these attributes warm and motivate the Water of the quantum Great Soul Lake. Without that heat, it would be the equivalent of ice.

Just a brief comparison of love in the three Water signs:

Cancer rules the most personal and early emotions, family emotions, and mothering. It represents the unconditional love of a parent, particularly a mother, for a child. So this is personal love.

Scorpio rules the emotions and exchanges between two people in a romantic relationship. Given a deep and lengthy experience, this can reach unconditional love, but Scorpio does not get there easily. The potential for betrayal, pain, and loss make this treacherous and bewildering territory. This is interpersonal love.

Pisces rules the unconditional love that supposedly exists in the areas of consciousness beyond the personal. This love is within the spiritual dimensions of nature, the universe, and the cosmos, and is what astrology calls transpersonal love.

~ CANCER ~
Water Zodiac Sign

Glyph ♋
Fourth Sign of the Zodiac Belt
Lowest Water Sign
"I nurture"
Ruled by Moon
Symbol is the Crab

This chapter does not refer to Cancer as a Sun sign but to the Cancer energy that exists in all of us to a degree. Cancerians or the Cancer types discussed here simply have more of it than most.

If we look at the zodiac belt from start to finish, from the first sign to the last, we see a progression that is like a metaphor for the life of a human. From Aries energy, bursting with zest to exist. To Taurus where we find we have a body. To Gemini, where we notice and register things, organize thought and store information. And then to the Water zodiac sign of Cancer where, according to the textbooks, we get our first experience of love—and naturally that means love from our parents, siblings, or main caregivers.

But why does Water come into the mix so late? Surely we are experiencing love from our parents when we are one hour old? Shouldn't the emotional zodiac sign be after Aries?

No, because, although we receive love from the beginning, we are not giving it back or manipulating it. We are in an instinctive, developing state with simple, primitive reflexes only, and the mind has no control over the body and its movements. Over the next months we start to develop and organize our knowledge banks, memory, and schemas—our Gemini skills. It is after this that we can recognize and organize sensitive experiences, emotions, and feelings.

So here we are at Cancer, and, as the first Water sign, it should be a fairly simple energy to grasp; usually the middle and higher signs get more complex. However, Water breaks that mould. Let's bring in some more head-scratchers and then see what all these jigsaw pieces mean in the context of the big picture.

According to the UK's National Lottery, the Cancer Sun sign is the most prevalent among the top winners. And Cancer Sun signs are joint third in the list of most common Sun signs among the world's wealthiest billionaires.

What's that? A retentive Water sign winning lotteries and becoming billionaires? Surely Fire is more likely to attract that kind of attention and luck? Things are starting to look as if they don't fit.

One explanation is that this is a Water sign with a "cardinal" overtone, and those two things together make it more powerful than the usual lowest zodiac sign of an Element. Before we can grasp what Cancer represents, we will have to understand what cardinal means.

The cardinal status is awarded to the four zodiac signs that are gatekeepers to four crucial points of the Sun's journey—the two solstices and the two equinoxes, each of which heralds a change in season.

Normally the cardinal status is easy to spot because, like the Masculine polarity, it doesn't stay hidden. The cardinal zodiac signs have an overlay of Masculine-style cardinality that makes them purposeful and tenacious and causes them to instigate and initiate, taking obvious roles of leadership. But Cancer's Water Element, which normally makes zodiac signs quiet and reticent, distorts appearances.

This is your first lesson in "layering" one astrological quality over another and it is an essential skill in psychological astrology. Humans are normally complex and difficult to understand. Just using the example from above, we might be totally perplexed that a man so reserved and secretive can be determined enough to thwart all competition and ruthlessly build a billion-dollar empire. But with astrology we can delve deep into his character and uncover the secrets to his success.

So, in this simple example of a Cancer Sun billionaire, we have to take two energies into account: the strong leadership qualities of the powerful cardinal influence, and Water's intuition and psychic abilities. Our billionaire has the quiet ability to instinctively read people or situations in order to put himself in the best position possible. Water's secrecy and psychic intuition, mixed with the immense power and drive of the cardinal, is apparently paying off.

Now, okay, I have simplified that in order to enable a "reading," and there may well be other factors involved, but at this point in your studies this example will do fine. As for the lottery wins, you could now work that out for yourself. It appears Water's psychic abilities are paying off!

I'm going to bring in some of the textbook wisdom on Cancer at this point. We are told Cancer types are "manipulative," but this word implies that they are scheming or devious and I wouldn't say that was true. It is more that they prefer subtle moves to directness. Just like a crab, Cancer energy moves sideways instead of going directly for something. This has the interesting result of confusing others; the Cancer-type person looks like they are going for something else, and they might even feign interest in it, creating a diversion. Then the big claw grabs the real target.

The result is that, for all their apparent softness, they will suddenly do something you didn't expect. Suddenly back out of a plan or even break a promise without so much as a by-your-leave or an explanation. And of course, they are not going to explain themselves—this is a non-verbal Water sign, so their defence is the unanswered telephone.

Cancerian empathy makes them good listeners and nurturers. They are naturally attuned to the pain, problems, and emotions of others, and those souls are drawn to the Cancerian obvious empathy. The Cancerian radar gently probes, searches, and listens to others with deep interest, because their stories, pain, and hopelessness are fascinating to Cancer's own emotional biases, and they love the deeply nurturing exchange.

Maybe surprisingly, they are often well-read and knowledgeable. They have a broad interest in most things and a curious intelligence. Sit them next to a garage mechanic, a court clerk, a gardening enthusiast, and a wine merchant and they will have something to discuss with all of them, such is the breadth of their knowledge and their interest in others.

But for all that, Cancer crabs are self-contained, and unlikely to reveal their own sensitivity and weaknesses. Their hurt is too deep and painful to be revealed to anyone. Cancer is intensely vulnerable to rejection, humiliation, and other people's opinions, so they hide it all away, appearing cool and composed in front of others.

It seems that this sentimental energy is the keeper of the family memories, be they on celluloid film or in photograph albums. The past, the roots, the home, mothering, and the idea of "mother" are all important. We are told that crabs hang on, and so does the Cancer energy—to home, security, people, and the family.

It is rare that a strongly Cancerian parent would split up a home or family, no matter what happens. They may be the most unhappy person on Earth, unloved and unloving, but nevertheless it is almost impossible for them to abandon the family home. Emotionally they will still be in it, long after their partner has left them, moved on, and remarried and the house has been sold. Still, in the heart of the Cancerian, is the determined belief that the partner will come back and they can become a family once more.

It is not unusual for them to live in the past, going over old loves or personal mistakes. However, they wouldn't want to discuss any of these things. Pain, secrets, and general disappointments are always well hidden. Most importantly, the family name is protected and all are spoken well of. Family skeletons are kept firmly in the cupboard and family problems are never discussed, even with the family.

It goes without saying that they are good with children and crusaders for their protection. Fostering comes easy to Cancerians, and rewards them with intense feelings of love for the orphans in their care. Cancer will reach out and find broken, disabled, and unwanted children, as well as pets, and anything else it can mother.

Moon Fact

In astrology the Moon is called a "planet" and it has a capital letter because "Moon" is its name.

Let's look at another unique feature of Cancer's world. Each zodiac sign has a planetary ruler, and for Cancer that is the Moon, which is special and different. First of all, it revolves round the Earth not the Sun, so that puts it into a class of its own. And from our perspective here on Earth it moves around the whole zodiac belt in roughly 28 days, whereas the fastest planets will take roughly a year.

So, Cancerians have a planetary ruler that experiences all zodiac signs and all planets in one month. That is an awful lot of symbolic life experience and it is what gives them their broad range of knowledge and interests.

Moon Fact

In the Egyptian sculpture of the zodiac in the Dendera Temple the symbol for Cancer is a crab, but carved as a round Moon disc with the correct number of five legs each side. Crabs actually prefer to move sideways so the legs don't get caught up in each other, so the shape and movement of the Dendera crab is a reminder of the Moon, which looks as if it has shifted to the left with every successive daily appearance. This fascinated the Ancient Egyptians, who are well known for their Sun worship, but not so much their Moon worship. As it happens, we can successfully draw a comparison between the Moon, the Cancer energy and the crab's nature with this.

As you will remember from your school days, the Moon's gravity raises the height of the Earth's ocean below it by sucking the seawater towards itself. Or, putting that another way, the Earth's tides are caused by the Moon's gravity. The Cancerian nature can also be "tidal" in that it ebbs and flows with strong currents and weaker swirls. It moves in and moves out according to the Moon's gravitational pushing or pulling.

The importance placed on the Moon by the cultures that lived around the eastern Mediterranean area is not understood in the West today. But over centuries and millennia, Moon cults and Sun cults fought over which was the more dominant, the Sun or the Moon. Walk through the British Museum to get a good impression of how important the Moon was from the sheer number of bull figurines. There are lion and horse statues too, representing the Sun, but not as many.

Looking at all this evidence, I am left with the impression that 2,000 years ago, the Moon had equal status to the Sun. And by association, Cancer must have been important too. Why have we forgotten this?

Because we have devalued the Feminine. For hundreds of years

Masculine energies have been favoured by societies and cultures. Science and academia are prized, while psychic and metaphysical skills are scorned. And let's not start on the opinion males in particular have of astrology! Cancer's Watery gifts are neat and undiluted; this is the most sensitive of all the Water signs. Their ability to "read" people, animals, and situations is astonishing, but this ability is usually well hidden, or entirely buried so that even *they* have no idea of their skills. As children, Cancerians are told their intuitive gifts are rubbish, and are scorned or frightened by the opinions of peers and adults. The soul hides its nervousness, its soft and caring feelings, the ready tears and genuine fears of being trodden on, and in with that burial go intuition, psychic awareness, and insight. These days, the Cancer energy available to our conscious selves amounts to the tip of the Cancer iceberg. We work with very little; the rest is hidden, boxed up, lashed down, and buried underwater—where our little crab is quite happy actually. The problem belongs to the human who is missing important parts of their birth chart. Learning all this is the first step to recovering them.

~ SCORPIO ~
Water Zodiac Sign

Glyph ♏
Eighth Sign of the Zodiac Belt
Middle Water Sign
"I desire"
Ruled by Pluto
Symbol is the Scorpion

This chapter does not refer to Scorpio as a Sun sign but to the Scorpio energy that exists in all of us to a degree. Scorpios or the Scorpio types discussed here simply have more of it than most.

The Scorpio energy is secretive but also possessive, which must be a tough double act. Surely if you are possessive then you show your hand and then the secret is out. But Scorpio can be most anything it wants to be.

Scorpio-type people are intensely private and deeply sensitive. They can be consciously aware of, or instinctively psychic to, things no one else sees, but they prefer to keep all that to themselves. At the very least, they are profoundly sensitive, with an internal radar system that misses nothing.

Their quietly charming, magnetic quality gives rise to the rumours of mysticism and the hushed awe we attach to Scorpio. This all adds to the curiosity and fear surrounding this charismatic, fascinating sign.

It might be useful to look at a myth from Genesis in the Old Testament regarding that version of creation. The winged, cunning serpent in the garden of Eden was "subtle," and "beguiled" Eve into eating the fruit from the forbidden tree. This metaphor, called original sin, obviously resulted in Adam's seduction and their eviction from Heaven or Eden. This biblical myth is so Scorpionic in nature. It transformed Adam and Eve's lives from immortal, ever-lasting, heavenly ones to earthly ones, with a future of sexual reproduction and physical death, a truly Scorpionic story.

I won't tiptoe around: Scorpio rules sex, violence, rape, incest, mating, reproductive, and intestinal processes. Its ruler is associated with birth and death. It harbours so much wrong-doing—and also, so much right-doing. But the wrongs can be so wrong. The Scorpio energy is unflinching as it navigates harrowing and depraved acts. If a human can come up with it, then one of the zodiac signs is harbouring it. And if it is not a suitable subject to discuss over afternoon tea, then it will be in the Scorpio energy.

When positively expressed, this sign has great power for the healing of the self and others. The energy *itself*, has a deep knowledge and mastery of the collective shadow or Underworld. Remember, I am not talking about the Sun sign; this is a description of the Scorpio energy only. So if a person is born with planets in Scorpio in their birth chart, they can, if they wish to, access their deep knowledge of these other planes of existence.

Scorpio represents the evolutionary force in nature that moves it to evolve, grow, and constantly seek to improve and gain power over the environment. And while we are thinking about the primordial, this energy also represents our deepest emotional responses and impulses of an animalistic nature, those driven by primitive reflexes.

In the past, miraculous healing and magical feats were attributed to this energy. It is also associated with transformation or death and resurrection into higher consciousness. Along with the other Water signs, it contains "codes of life," but Scorpio takes that further . . . much, much further. Into places that most humans get embarrassed about.

It is associated with the transformation that occurs on a soul level when we become intimately bonded with another sexually, and not just because of the always present potential for pregnancy, which is, of course, the biggest transformation of all. This energy suggests that sexual intercourse changes something within the individual, even if it is not recognized.

However, the separation of religion from the pagan, natural world over the last 2,000 years has meant that sex has become a smutty, humiliating, taboo subject. Consequently, we have completely lost touch with the most sacred, spiritual truth of all time. Occasionally this is alluded to in culture. I remember a line from a Kate Bush song in the late 1970s, "sex is the root of our incarnations;" and around 900 CE, Hindus were being taught in tantra that "Desire is the root of the universe."

At the heart of Scorpio is the knowledge that the intimacy of coitus between two consensual partners can access a spiritual experience of ecstatic, other-dimensional qualities. This dissolves the barriers to true spiritual enlightenment, allowing recognition of the ultimate and supreme cosmic truth—that everything in our dimension is built around bringing the two halves together. Libra's world of two becomes one again.

That sounds quite simple, but it needs thinking about. In spiritual terms the two halves could be yang and yin or Masculine and Feminine. In scientific terms it could be matter, and its electrical opposite—antimatter. Bringing those two together results in a big, galactic bang and the release of large quantities of energy—much like the type of sex Scorpio enjoys.

There are many different ways to consider this joining of the two halves and just one of them is in the structure of astrology on page 12, which doesn't just demonstrate the splitting of those two components into the smaller packets of zodiac signs. It also demonstrates the route *back to unity*, the blending into oneness once more, where all is merged into sublime, ecstatic intensity and the euphoria of completeness.

The Western seeker of communion with divine spirit, or a peak spiritual experience, might like to know that sex is where Hinduism and other cultures found it in centuries and millennia past, and this knowledge has formed the basis of all religious and spiritual doctrine ever since, although no self-respecting religion would ever consider that.

This sacred knowledge was where humans could experience the sublime coming together of the two polar opposites (yin/Feminine and yang/Masculine) in the spiritual perfection that exists at the very heart of the invisible cosmos. The same state as the original singularity, before the Big Bang. The only place humans can experience intense oneness; in mythological terms the sacred melding of Heaven and Earth, when Ouranos joins with Gaia. (I'm not leaving out any sexual preferences here; in same-sex couples there is always one yin and one yang character. Gaia can just as easily be a gender male or Ouranos a gender female.)

These ideas are not new. Indologist and historian Alain Daniélou wrote of them after considerable research into Hindu cosmology, which, interestingly, also embraces astrology. For Daniélou the world is based on two opposite poles, akin to the Masculine creative principle and the Feminine process. The union of these two, or any other duality, creates a state of pacified bliss and an experience of the Absolute.

Now I want to focus on the word "intensity." Scorpio is intense, and also extreme, fervent, fierce, forceful, and passionate. So I want to make a comparison between the intensity of the feeling nature of the Scorpionic person and the intensity of an orgasm. It is about time somebody pointed out that these two intensities are comparable, so that we get a better understanding of the Scorpio energy.

I suppose it is unsurprising that when it comes to relationships, Scorpionic people usually need to delve deeply into the other person. If they like someone, they can't help but get closer and closer, with long, penetrating eye contact and piercing attentiveness. As you can imagine, this tends to go down well with prospective lovers, and Scorpionic people often don't struggle to find romantic companions.

However, trust is a big issue. To start with, every single word and action of a potential lover is analyzed for the sole purpose of uncovering that which is hidden, to make sure that this person is what they seem. There are good reasons for this: the Scorpio-type person knows how very vulnerable they can be when it comes to their emotions, which are powerfully intense and very demanding for all concerned. They will eventually attach to their lover in a very committed and deep way with feelings of love, loyalty, and devotion. These are generated during sexual activity, which engages them in a profound way, even though they will never speak of it.

The lack of trust initially is because they are so hypersensitive to betrayal, they can't re-trust if let down. They can be possessive of loved ones and prone to jealousy, which is entirely down to the intensity they feel. They don't tolerate flirts and they do not forgive indiscretions. If they suspect any kind of disloyalty, they end the relationship and it can never be recovered. The end is final.

Having said that, sometimes they are forced to remain in the relationship for other compelling reasons. Then they will become cold and hard, withdrawing from the bedroom and sleeping alone for the rest of their lives if necessary. Any semblance of love, affection, or desire will disappear faster than a snowball in a fire, with no chance of things returning to how they were. And there is no place lonelier than the frosty atmosphere around the Scorpion that has discovered treachery.

I'm afraid all the above includes relationships with platonic friends too; they must also be loyal above all else. Scorpio-type people do not like finding out they have been gossiped about, so their friends should be careful not to reveal their secrets.

When sex with the current partner becomes impossible because of betrayal, then Scorpionic males, in particular, may be unfaithful themselves.

They need deeply transformative sex to survive and feel alive, so once this is not available in their relationship they will unconsciously and instinctively seek it anywhere they can get it. This may mean all the crisis of a triangle, but it is preferable to the two alternatives—sex with a partner who deceived them or no sex at all.

Scorpio-type people have control needs that are based on the fears we looked at earlier. However, they can't control what they *feel*, they can only control what others see. And they sure do control that. They also want to control when and where initial intimacies take place and may not like the prospective partner taking the lead.

All this controlling can make them appear moody, but they don't consider themselves moody, more thoughtful. They are often serious and lack humour. If you remember, Water is good at deliberately manipulating atmosphere, but this can also happen without any intention to do so. Somehow, without them even knowing it, a heavy and uncomfortable atmosphere can seep through the house, making everyone else want to slam doors and smash plates. Scorpions may not make emotional scenes themselves, but they manage to create emotional responses in others.

This is certainly an energy to watch out for. In the Scorpio dark side lurks the occasional Voldemort whose release can be enabled by an ego-inflating Fire energy. Such a combination can become abusive, malefic, or destructive. This sort of character is best given a wide berth.

When it comes to career choices, there a few that stand out. Some are obvious, like digging deeply into the Earth to discover things—drain engineering, mining, and forensic crime investigation. On the far-fetched side, can you imagine James Bond being a Scorpio-type? Surely all that subterfuge and secrecy would appeal to him. I suspect there are a fair few surgeons with Scorpionic traits, "going in deep" with a scalpel. And then there is psychology and psychiatry—exploring the mind without a scalpel. I once had the pleasure of knowing the manager of an emergency hostel for rape and domestic violence victims, with three planets in Scorpio. And of course, funeral parlours and crematoriums will resonate with Scorpio because of the death and transitioning theme.

I haven't talked much about the opposite Sign of Taurus, so we really do need to cover the key words of this opposition to start to get an understanding of it. According to traditional astrology, money is an issue for both these signs. Taurus because it is an Earth sign and protective about its financial security. Scorpio's motive is a little more opaque. Money is a reward, seen as the result of success and achievement, and it certainly invokes all kinds of treachery and subterfuge. It can excite, cause jealousy and family wars, and create spectacularly bloodthirsty divorces. Just the kind of tangled emotional vipers' nest that attracts Scorpio energy, one way or another.

So we find those with a Scorpio midheaven working as divorce lawyers, financial consultants specialising in hiding money, or, strangely, in banks, handling other people's money. I suppose the uncompromising thoroughness and commitment is a good fit for a bank—but we will come across more clues when we look at houses.

All things quantum, nuclear, and subatomic are ruled by Pluto, and by association Scorpio too, including the unmentionables, such as genetic engineering and eugenics. This is the underside to nature and the invisible three-dimensional web that underpins life itself (see page 47).

Scorpio can summon serpent power for healing, and it certainly contains the healing gifts found in Water. However, there is a difference between Scorpio's healing and that of Cancer and Pisces, which is unconditional. In Scorpio's case it is time-limited and conditional.

This is to do with Scorpio's harsher nature and unflinching attitude to death. As a Water sign, Scorpio will offer sympathy and understanding for a while, but the wounded are expected to take part in their own recovery and no messing. Scorpio will assist in the change and transformation that is most likely needed, but will not wait around while the victim keeps returning to the addiction, be it an abusive boyfriend, alcohol, sugar, smoking, drugs, or whatever else.

~ PISCES ~

Water Zodiac Sign

Glyph ♓
Twelfth Sign and Last Sign of the Zodiac Belt
Highest Water Sign
"I yearn"
Ruled by Neptune
Symbol is Two Fishes

This chapter does not refer to Pisces as a Sun sign but to the Pisces energy that exists in all of us to a degree. Pisceans or the Pisces types discussed here simply have more of it than most.

This elusive and gentle energy is hard to grasp and harder to describe, for it can be almost anything you want. Piscean people will morph before your eyes into what you need, and will be what you long for. Their kind and tender demeanour can melt the hardest heart, and they will soon have you convinced your dreams can come true.

Below is a word list from a dictionary. The words are all important, so don't just glance over it; read it out and consider each word, then you'll be halfway to knowing this energy. This book is about the easiest way to learn astrology and this is the easiest way to learn about Pisces. The word "imaginary" means: assumed, chimerical, dreamt, fanciful, fictional, hallucinatory, ideal, illusive, illusory, imagined, phantasmal, shadowy, visionary, fantasized, conjured, whimsical, inspired, subjective, creative, and, finally, insightful. Every single one of those words describes the Pisces energy!

Because this sign is the last in the zodiac it is literally "tired." It represents the dissolving of our humanness and the return to the Great Soul Lake, or "dark" (meaning invisible) matter outside of our dimension. To leave Earth and "go home," to the cosmic memory held in the Great Soul Lake or dark matter. Because it is a Water sign it looks to the past, as they all do, but it also heeds the call to *dissolve* everything. To take all experience, pain, and learning into the equivalent of a primordial soup.

The first problem we come across in Pisces-land is the lack of boundaries. If your energy is about dissolving all structures, defences, and convictions, ready for the development of new beginnings, then you have no limits, which has quite an impact on life.

First of all, Pisces can't say "no" to anyone, and they will attempt to meet every request and plea, no matter how much trouble it will land them in. Add to this that they will always say what the person in front of them wants to hear. Anything they promised to anyone previously gets lost in the mist of yesterday, and all they hear and see is this person, right here, right now, whom they must serve. Their skin is porous and their energy is highly sensitive to the needs of others, especially those right in front of them, so *they* come first and the others are forgotten.

A lack of boundaries in a romantic relationship can lead to a few more problems. The need to do what the partner wants takes over their lives to the point where they can't find their own mind . . . which wasn't particularly important to them anyway. Sometimes they are so aware of pleasing the significant other they take their cues from them or copy them, and lose their own personal identity. If the partner is a strong Fire person this works fine—the two bits of jigsaw fit perfectly, one full of ego, the other ego-less. Air signs might struggle for space though.

Some of the nicest features include their ability to mop up all the toxicity, aggression, and bad stuff like a sponge. Their compassion really is endless and totally unconditional. They try to help in the places angels would fear to tread.

Christian mythology is resonant with the Piscean theme. Their Bible tells us Jesus loved the world so much, he gave his life for the sake of humanity. The messiah also had strong associations with healing, helping the poor and deprived, psychic or prophesizing abilities, pacifism, being non-judgemental, and being welcoming to outcasts. I certainly think making this association helps us to understand Pisces.

The Piscean energy looks beyond mortality into the cosmos and the Great White Light for its home. It feels compassion for the whole world and everyone in it. The human ego (Fire Element) becomes unimportant after Sagittarius, the ninth zodiac sign. The last three signs (Capricorn, Aquarius, Pisces) demonstrate interests outside of individuating and a diminishing interest in feeling personally important.

Pisces knows with some certainty that the individual ego now has to give itself up for the greater good; its time is done, and all that it strove for no longer matters.

Piscean-type people are what we might term "very old souls." They have vague memories that don't really fit with life here on Earth. Some of these memories might be about the cosmic soup that existed before our dimension, when all was just blissful oneness, before strange things happened to the quantum particles and they began to form primordial matter in a great Big Bang. The next thing that Pisces is aware of is this dimension, with its harsh structures and separation.

But somewhere inside the Pisces energy is the memory of the all-encompassing love of the supreme cosmos and the perfect purity of the Great White Light.

So, Pisces longs and pines and yearns to return to that utopian kingdom of nirvana, pure love, and unity with the divine source. And Pisces-type people also feel an enormous guilt for how things turned out. Did they do something wrong? OMG, what if they pressed the wrong button or something? Hence, Pisces wants to make up for it, to redeem itself and do good; to put the whole thing right again, to bring us back to this place of loving unity.

Some Pisceans might not get as far as identifying primordial, cosmic mistakes, so they might personalize the same feeling into a yearning for a disenchanted lover who is now unreachable, or long for a successful football team when the one they support never wins. Perhaps the pining could be for five correct numbers in the lottery, or just another bottle of whisky to drink all into blissful oblivion.

Alcohol and drugs are a popular escape for them as so many don't really like living in the real world. If only they could just go back . . .

Their lives can be quite chaotic as they get tossed around on a sea of dilemmas and problems, but Pisces has endless compassion and devotion to share with all who need it. They never stop believing in people and ideals, despite the experience of regular disappointments and all evidence to the contrary. Listen out for the words "It doesn't matter"—meaning it is of no consequence; but also consider matter as in material things, which are of little value to Piscean energy. They are at their happiest when devoted to a cause or helping people.

This is also true of their opposite sign, Virgo, because this whole opposition is dedicated to, among other things, service to others and health services.

As a Water sign, you'd think they would be good with relationships, but no, Pisces is one of the last four transpersonal signs, and as such has moved out of the relationship or interpersonal section of the zodiac belt. It is not that they don't have, or enjoy relationships, they do, they are just not very adapted to them—or very good at them.

Time is very much a feature of our dimension, probably because it is a measure of matter and material things degrading. We are mortal and so age over time. Things on the other side or in other dimensions are immortal, hence they are going to last for ever; therefore, time isn't important to Piscean types.

The Earth signs are usually capable of managing time and Virgo is quite pernickety about it, but Pisces struggles. Their timing in relationships is often way off; either they declare their love too soon and scare their partner off, or not at all and the partner gets fed up with waiting. Pisces can be a disaster when choosing the appropriate moment to talk about love.

They seem to like falling in love—the giddy euphoria resonates with their dreamy, soft, imaginative nature, so it happens quite easily. However, going back to their lack of boundaries and free love ethics, they can adore being in love so much they forget they are already married! Some are barely monogamous and have a new love in their sights before leaving the old one. Big fights and emotional scenes upset them deeply, so they don't like to discard lovers; that would hurt them. But it doesn't stop them from falling in love with number two and getting into worse trouble in a triangle! Multiple loves can often suit the Piscean habit of having someone to yearn for and pine after. When they are with one, they can pine after the other.

Or they go the other way and become completely besotted with one person who is geographically, emotionally, or physically unavailable. In this case they don't need a second love; because the first one is always so totally unavailable, they can—and do—yearn to their heart's content. As usual with Water signs, Piscean-type people would like to fuse with the beloved and climb into their skin. Singer/songwriter Darren Hayes, who has Moon in Pisces, writes beautiful and oh, so Piscean songs in which he declares that he loved partners before he even met them and how he longs to be their only wish and fantasy. In return, he will love them more with every breath.

Love suits Pisces types' dreamy nature; they just climb in the boat and float down the stream in a haze of euphoria. They are quite capable of picking someone completely unsuitable, even abusive, unavailable, emotionally unstable, borderline, and then just staying in there, long after any sane person would have given up, believing, and believing, that one day the beloved will change . . .

Putting lovers aside, this is generally a zodiac sign that wants to include the world and does not like to give attention to just one person. They will be kind and considerate and aim to please the people they meet, but then give the same attention to an impoverished tramp or someone waiting in the bus queue. They are full of big inconsistencies when it comes to relating. Yes, there will be times of slavish devotion, but then they will offer the same to all their neighbours. Pisceans don't like to think one person is getting all the attention.

Piscean energy tends to get very tired and needs to sleep a lot. They like bouts of lazing in the shallows. This is because their nervous systems are very porous and sensitive; they can't take the workloads of Capricorn and Virgo. The no-boundaries thing relates to their bodies too; it can seem that their very cells are under attack from the cosmic energies at the edges of our world—their immune systems especially come under fire from allergies and autoimmune irritations. I have known more than a few have vague, difficult-to-diagnose symptoms that confound all the testing and then after a while simply disappear.

An impressive natural acting ability comes from their ability to morph into anyone. The lack of need to strengthen their own egos during their lifetime means they can relax, they have nothing they need to fight for. Hence, they can be poured into any container. This only becomes a problem when several people are asking for just this, all at the same time. That's when those slippery scales come in handy, as none can catch the elusive fish as it slides away . . .

Being in Your Element

Ever heard the saying "in their element?" It actually comes from old astrology of many centuries ago. It is used when we mean someone is happily attuned to their environment; and we say "out of their element" when someone is doing something alien to their true calling.

The best way to understand how we can help or sabotage a feeling of well-being is look at an example. The birth chart could show that a person is blessed with a lot of Fire energy. This should make them energetic, rather obvious, and confident. Aha, but what if they are morose, despondent, and lifeless? Well, stuff happens, but, as we shall see, there are always ways to help us feel better once we start trusting astrology.

The spiritual essence of the Elements in our psychological profile can be reached by using their physical counterparts. Seriously. Physical water, the H_2O stuff, can actually absorb human emotions. It is worth looking online for the work of Masaru Emoto: He was convinced that human consciousness could affect the molecular structure of water and took photographs to support his theory.

So . . . going back to the lifeless Fire Element person—they need the presence of real fire to feel better. Fire signs should appreciate the Sun, candles, or a hearth fire. The real flames will warm their spirits.

Likewise, Water signs should feel content in or on water—rain, oceans, rivers, canals, pools, or even a bath. The molecules of water somehow "absorb" excess emotion or, conversely, encourage an emotional response. Either way, this comforts the soul, which is itself a Water entity.

For Air signs, it is actually the exhilaration of height and a wide, open sky. Mono-gliding, sky-diving, or mountain climbing will get them "in their element." Aircraft may not, since the windows are tiny and the view restricted. This environment may actually be claustrophobic because there is a possibility of feeling trapped. The person will be aware that they cannot control the way out.

Earth signs should find it easier to get a good match. They just need a garden with clay pots. Owning earthly things is important—homes, cars, pension funds, etc. I have even watched Earth signs look through bank statements for a sense of well-being! We are all different it seems.

Sorting the Zodiac Signs into Different Groups

Well, this is exciting! You have reached your first milestone. You have a basic understanding of the zodiac signs. Great news. Now the not-so-good news—there is more to learn about these **psychological forces or energies**. I'm going to sort them into different groups so we can make comparisons. Hopefully, you have remembered that the zodiac signs "colour" the meaning of the planet as it travels through that segment of the sky around us? Good! And hopefully you have learned all your glyphs too? Bravo!

Now we are going to look at the zodiac belt in a NATURAL wheel.

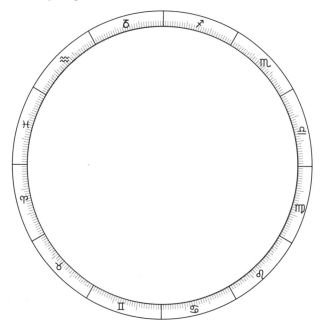

Fig. 10: The Zodiac Belt on a Natural Wheel

Note that the image of this natural wheel is used for teaching purposes and astrology cannot be read from it.

Look for Aries on the left-hand side, then Taurus underneath that. Keep going in the same anticlockwise direction, reading them all out and getting used to what comes after what.

We are going to learn about three different groupings. Each of these will give you even more information about these psychological forces or energies.

Just a quick word first! Don't get put off by any unknown words and "jargon" used here. You don't need jargon to read a birth chart; but it will be useful for you to know what it is when you read it in astrology sources online. First and foremost, you need to know the meanings of the glyphs on the birth chart and that's it.

The Quadruplicities or Modalities

Quadruplicity means four in a group. So, twelve signs, with four in a group, means three groups. The groups are called **cardinal**, **fixed**, and **mutable**.

The Cardinal Signs

The cardinal signs are Aries (Fire), Capricorn (Earth), Libra (Air), and Cancer (Water).

You should note from this that in cardinality there is one sign from each Element. Have a look at Figure 10 and put a finger on each of those four signs so you get used to where they are compared to the others in the same group.

Cardinal energy proceeds outwards. It initiates. All four of these zodiac signs pursue their needs and goals and try to persuade others to do the same. They are self-motivated and natural leaders, so they want to pick up the baton and run with it. The cardinal modality or overlay at least tries to do something, and will attempt to instigate corrections or deal with matters.

However, they all reach for the ideals of their *own Element*, and clash with the other three in the group. Let's look at a couple of examples:

Aries exhilarates in combat and crusading, but Cancer always seeks a peaceful, loving path. So Aries thinks Cancer is a wimpish, cowardly energy while Cancer thinks Aries is bloodthirsty and brutal.

Libra is social and willing to spend on decorations, but Capricorn dislikes frivolous ornaments, preferring to spend on useful tools. Those two would have difficulty coming to an agreement on the number of hours that Capricorn works, how much socialising Libra likes to do, and how the house should be decorated.

The cardinals have a Masculine-style overlay, which leads outwards and forwards in straight lines. Aries and Libra are Masculine energy anyway; hence the cardinal overlay produces the formidable forces of opposite signs Aries and Libra.

However, Cancer and Capricorn, which are also opposite signs, are both from the Feminine polarity, so when the cardinal (Masculine-style) overlays them, things could get more complicated. We have looked at what happens to Cancer, so I won't repeat that one. Meanwhile, Capricorn's position as the highest Earth Element sign favours the status of the Masculine overlay, which makes it more authoritative and controlling.

Cardinality and Masculinity are compatible. When they are not, as with Cancer (Femininity) and cardinality, it is difficult for that person to feel comfortable. One energy is trying to be more assertive, the other wants to run and hide.

The Fixed Signs

The fixed signs are Taurus (Earth), Leo (Fire), Scorpio (Water), and Aquarius (Air).

You will note that one sign from each of the Elements is fixed. Go back to Figure 10 and have a look at where they all are. You will see that those four signs make up a cross shape.

Fixed energy, as the name suggests, does not want to change anything. I imagine each of these signs to have a tube of everlasting, unmoveable glue that they apply to circumstances, friends, and belongings. Great if loyalty and endurance are called for; but a problem if a partner wants an end to the relationship.

Even if stuck in a rut, they will not let go, and have a great deal of strength in their resistance to change. They do this by simply staying put, by planting two feet down and not moving. However, although they won't be pushed around, they will not willingly trample on somebody else's ground either. They aren't particularly aggressive in this; it is more the case that they become immobile or just stop where they are.

This type of determination can be useful—what somebody else has started, they will follow through to the bitter end. Their lives can be about stability, consistency, perseverance, and preservation. However, if you are on the receiving end of all these virtues, it sure feels like stubbornness!

Notice also the heavy central gravity or magnetism, which draws people to them.

Aquarius and Leo have the most difficulty dealing with this overlay of fixed energy. Their Masculine nature instructs them to move boldly forward while the fixity pours concrete around their boots. Most manage this inner "personality clash" by telling everyone else where they are going wrong and how much they should change. In the meantime, they have difficulty entertaining the thought of a new route to work.

The Mutable Signs

The mutable signs are Gemini (Air), Virgo (Earth), Sagittarius (Fire), and Pisces (Water).

As before, go back to Figure 10 and find those remaining signs. They also form a four-pointed cross. The Masculine axis of Air/Gemini and Fire/Sagittarius is crossed by the Feminine axis of Water/Pisces and Earth/Virgo.

The mutable signs come after the immoveable dead weight of the fixed signs and it is their job to crack open that concrete and get things moving again. And they do this in such different ways. Virgo fidgets and shakes with worry, Gemini constantly moves position in any direction, shimmering Pisces shape-shifts, and Sagittarius journeys outwards in relentless questing for distant truths.

However, they are all restless and changeable, which is good, because they have to mediate between the immoveable persistence of the fixed signs and the unstoppable force of cardinal signs.

They are adjustable, flexible, and restless, not forceful or persistent. Even though Sagittarius is "always right" and communicates this quite forcefully, it will quickly move away from those things that irritate it and be over the horizon with great speed. They tend to serve, and even Sagittarius serves when it is teaching—although that is as close as it gets to service!

There is a great deal of movement associated with these signs. Going through them again—Gemini gets restless and bored. Sagittarius just knows that the grass is always greener on the other side and they follow their dreams. Virgo is always restless and twitching with worry; their minds are forever going over stuff. Pisces ceaselessly swims around and moves with the great ocean of the cosmic ether—another dreamy energy following yearnings and longings for who-knows-what.

Generally, mutable signs are not particularly bothered by change (although Virgo is bothered by everything). Quite often they are accused of inconsistency and that would be correct, although they would see it as being fluid and adaptable.

They will find their way around things and avoid conflict, unless it is to mediate or reconcile. Maybe there is more interest in the journey than the destination!

The Triplicity, or Signs in the Same Element

You can now breathe a sigh of relief because you already know this one! The section on the 12 zodiac signs was divided into the four Elements. So each of the four groups in the triplicities has the three signs of the same element. Can you remember them?

The Fire signs—Aries, Leo, and Sagittarius
The Earth signs—Taurus, Virgo, and Capricorn
The Air signs—Gemini, Libra, and Aquarius
The Water signs—Cancer, Scorpio, and Pisces

Go back to Figure 10 and find the position of each sign in those groups. Each group makes a triangle shape in the wheel.

You will read astrology books telling you that the triplicities are harmonious and get on well. I'm not so sure. They might share the same way of doing something, but that doesn't necessarily mean they appreciate each other. Let's just take the Fire signs. They have been asked to make a presentation together. And who is going to do the most speaking and who is going to plan the campaign, make the tea, and clear up the big mess afterwards? (These are Fire signs, there will be a big mess!) Obviously, Aries will want to organize the whole thing their way, from content to lighting. Leo and Sagittarius will be pushing each other out of the way to get on the stage, and no one will make the tea or clear up. Harmonious? I don't think so!

Opposite Signs, Two in a Group

SIGN	OPPOSITE SIGN
Aries Masculine Fire My needs. Asserting self. Glory of battle.	Libra Masculine Air Awareness of need of others. Striving for cooperation. Will resort to battle. Eye for an eye, tooth for a tooth.
Taurus Feminine Earth Intense physical feeling. Sensual, non-emotional merger. "Self"-centred, looking for self-gratification. Personal possessions.	Scorpio Feminine Water Intense emotional feeling. Erotic, emotional merger. The desire to be "joined" with, to own, or to "consume" another. Shared wealth.

Fig. 11: Opposite Signs

Gemini Masculine Air Lacking confidence. Knowing bits of knowledge and separate facts. Collecting and learning. Immature opinions.	**Sagittarius** Masculine Fire Confidence. Knowing from experience and knowledge. Forming beliefs, wisdom, faith, confidence, philosophy, law, and religion. Formed opinions.
Cancer Feminine Water Conserving. Unconditional love. Seeking security/insecure. Personal emotional needs. Gentle child-nurturing. No defences, need to hide. Sensitive.	**Capricorn** Feminine Earth Conserving. Conditional love. Building security. Unemotional. Nurturing status/success/ acquisition. Strong backbone. Hardened.
Leo Masculine Fire Recognition of self as all- important. Autocracy. Wants to be different/unique. Needs special attention. One's ego is special.	**Aquarius** Masculine Air No one person is important. The group is important. Democracy. Wants to be different/unique. Will not give special attention. No ego is special.

Fig. 11: Opposite Signs

Virgo Feminine Earth Health. Criticism/guilt. Cleansing process. Discriminates and labels the separate parts. Worries. It *matters*. Service. Serves. Detailed.	Pisces Feminine Water Health. Lethargy/guilt. Cleansing process. Dissolves everything into undifferentiated whole. No worries. It *doesn't matter*. Also serves, but as many as possible. Indifferent to detail.

Fig. 11: Opposite Signs

This section concludes the theory on zodiac signs. We have learnt how to look at them individually, in a partnership, as part of a group, as adversaries, and as components of a whole. Each of these energies is a part of yourself and a part of the universe we live in.

Keep reading over these pages and any of the books in the list at the end. You need to understand these forces and be able to recall information about them instantly.

Well done for getting this far. Just a few more pages and you will be reading astrology. And even more than this, because we are **diving deeply into the origins and structures underlying behaviour**, we are learning **behavioural psychological astrology**, which enables us to understand and modify behaviour and achieve happier outcomes.

The Houses of the Horoscope
How the Birth Chart Is Constructed

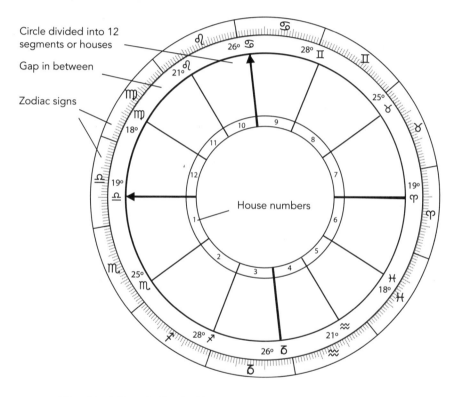

Fig. 12: A Simple Birth Chart with Houses and Zodiac Signs

My goodness, we are about to see our first proper birth chart. It might look a bit empty at this point, but there is sufficient here to do a pretty good reading. This may sound surprising, but **you do not need planets to practise astrology**.

This is the birth chart configuration.

The outer ring is the zodiac belt. (Remember that from Figure 10?) Inside that, there is a gap representing space. Then inside that you can see 12 segments (like a large cake, cut into uneven slices); these are called houses. They are completely separate to the zodiac signs.

You have learned the meanings of the zodiac signs, now you are going to learn about the meaning of the houses.

Each house represents a facet, side, part, or area of our lives. Perhaps that is worth repeating—each house represents a facet of our lives.

How the Zodiac Signs Spin round the Houses

The zodiac belt, made up of all the zodiac signs, now spins round the circle of houses and can land anywhere.

I am making this easy, and there is no reason to learn it any other way. You can catch up with all the highly technical stuff in time; right now, I don't want to put you off by complicating things. At this time, the only *essential* thing to know is how the zodiac signs slide round the houses and what that means.

To help understand this crucial dynamic, make a copy of the birth chart diagram in this book and cut the outer ring of zodiac signs off it. Put the rest in the middle and stabilize it. Now move the thin ring of zodiac signs around it. It can stop anywhere you want.

And THAT is the main mechanics of a birth chart. This is where the best part of your astrological information comes from; ignore everything else for the time being.

Birth charts can be designed in many different formats, depending on individual preference. So the style of a chart might be different when you see it online. However, we have teamed up with **astro.com**, where you will find a "chart drawing" or "natal chart wheel" that is just like the ones in this book. This will make things easier for the first part of your astrology journey. Get started on your first chart now by going to **astro.com** and registering. Then follow the step-by-step guide which can be found on page 168 and also on **www.alisonchesterlambert.com**.

Here are some things to note about Figure 12. The zodiac signs are all equal in size. Each one takes up 30 degrees of the full circle of 360 degrees. 12 x 30 = 360 degrees.

The houses are not so obliging; they can be any size from tiny to enormous. If it is a tiny house, it may only be a few degrees wide. Or it may be such a big house, let's say 72 degrees wide, that three zodiac signs may cover it. In which case that facet of your life holds a lot of opportunity!

As we learn about the houses, we will start to look at how the zodiac signs influence the duties of that house. The following wheel highlights the Masculine and Feminine houses and their elements.

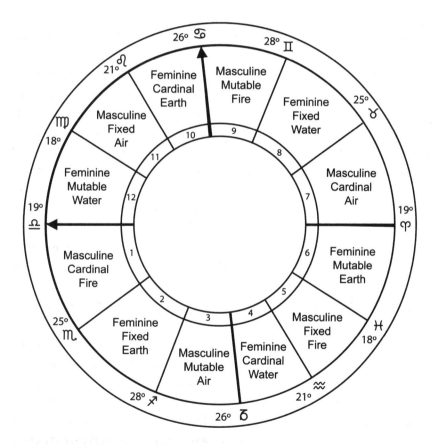

Fig. 13: House Diagram with Polarity, Quadruplicity, and Triplicity

The Meaning of the Masculine Fire Houses

The first, fifth, and ninth houses—or facets of our lives—are the Masculine Fire houses. You may want to reread the chapter on Fire energy before you read this, to refresh your memory.

Just like the Fire zodiac signs, the three Fire houses have Masculine-style energy that wants to burst into life and gobble up everything it can burn. These houses or facets of our lives are the areas in which we should find inspiration, optimism, and faith in the future. Together they represent our potential for confidence and joy, with an exciting enthusiasm for the future.

So if we want to find that special belief that we are "worth it," we should invoke the Fire facets of our life so our spirit can shine through. Remember that Fire always precedes Earth, so it is the raw impulse and fuel that precedes the manifestation of material things.

For some individuals, the possibilities of Fire's imagination can seem unachievable or silly. They still smart from all the times they were told to stop showing off! With their confidence shattered, they withdraw under a self-made glass ceiling, giving themselves no chance to reach for their magnificence. Why would any of us do that?

It all goes back to childhood and the colour our parents loved us in—a theory of mine that we looked at earlier. They loved us, that's for sure, but was the "colour" the right one for us?

If they loved us in red, then when we achieved something, they would have cheered and said, "You are amazing. How fantastic is that? Wow, let's take a photo!"

If they loved us in blue we would have heard, "Yes, very good, but if you had done such-and-such, it would have been more impressive." Or maybe they even ignored the success, saying, "Now get ready for dinner, wash your hands." (They got this blue love from their own parents!, so that's where they learned this response!)

If we got the red love, then we learned to be receptive to excited praise and **attention**, and now we have the confidence to reach even higher and believe we can do more. If we didn't get red, but blue instead, we learn to shrink back, getting the impression that it isn't good to show off and win. That lesson will still impact us, fifty years of failure later.

The answer? **Give yourself the red love.** Love your inner child and look to your Fire houses for the clues you need to claim your success and joy. The truth of the matter is that **this dimension is built on attention and belief.** One of the Mysteries of Ancient Greece was the knowledge that the gods cannot live without praise and worship. Within each of us is Fire and the spirit of deity, I know this because it is there in the birth chart.

Monotheistic religions have traditionally preached that we should be pious and humble, but that was to keep us in the audience while their representatives abused their superiority without even moral boundaries.

It is a legacy that leaves us small and embarrassed. Let me be clear. We cannot rise to our greatest heights without honouring our Fire/spirit and feeling the exhilaration of our specialness. Fire holds the vision of our future, so we can identify the possibilities and move confidently towards them. More importantly, Fire can imagine the future differently from what it is now, and it isn't held back by pessimism.

Unfortunately, there is little room to manoeuvre when it comes to honouring our Fire inheritance. You may think that you have buried your "undesirable Fire ego" in the depths of your Underworld or shadow, but it won't stay there for ever. And when it does erupt, you will have no control over it. You will also find it stressful to be around those who are happy to play their Fire, and that can make you miserable.

The First House

We have learned that it all begins with energy and that is the substance of the first house, because, after all, it is a Fire house. It is an energetic burst into life.

This house resonates with the raw vitality of Aries and Mars.

This facet of our lives is all about the spurt of energy and spirit needed to "arrive on the Earth." Rather like a firework, the first house pushes out into life. And whatever is in it, goes with it. So, if Libra is in the first house, then Libra bursts out.

If we look at the houses as a journey from the first to the twelfth, and that as a metaphor for the life of a human, then we start out as the totally self-centred baby, bursting onto life's stage in the delivery room of the first house. It is our immediate interaction with "life" and our life force. This is the "spirit" of us, and what others see first.

The zodiac sign in the first house may also describe a baby's birth. If Aries is in charge, it will have been fast, with instant attention demands. If Capricorn sits there, it will have been fearful for some reason, with hard work and a determination to get here.

There is no complexity or depth to this house; it is all about the will to exist and raw vitality. Just a simple, pure energy form, with no idea of the impact it has on others.

Do any of us see what the world sees when it looks at us? Not quite. We can never really see ourselves as others do. Our viewing and appreciation mechanism cannot separate enough to give us a good view. Do you recognise, or even like, your own voice if you hear a recorded version? Many people don't.

If we are a building then this house is our front door, our view of the world. People come to the door and we interact with them through it. They see this part of us first. Everything in the birth chart has to pass through this door. But still we can't see it ourselves, for we cannot separate ourselves from it; we cannot stand further away and look back at it with perspective.

The Fifth House

The Sun and Leo are associated with the fifth house, so what facet of our lives are we looking into with that as a clue? It is our "personal power" house and it describes our zest for life and happiness. When everything is right with this house, it is where we feel joy and cheerfulness. It is the area of our life where we can express ourselves and have some fun at the same time.

So obviously we find and create our personal power here; but we develop personal identity here too, which leads on to identifying our strengths and successes. This is where you can give your own inner child the red love I talked about in the Fire houses introduction. And you will never give yourself a greater gift.

The word "creation" is also used in association with the fifth. Often this means creating something to feel proud of, or a brilliant expression of oneself. This can be works of art or playwriting, a dramatic performance, or something of that nature. Do you delight in acting, or are you a good musician? Do you like knitting, online gaming, tapestry-making, or any kind of sport? Is there something that makes you feel great when you succeed at it? All these things matter so much to the divine within us, because we are exposing, and then glorying in, our prowess or sense of fun. We are finding the best bit of ourselves.

If we play with the word "creation," we can get re-creation, where something is done for enjoyment, and pro-creation, as in creating a child. Creating children is a fifth house thing? That used to mystify me. Then I was taught that it is because we can attempt to project our future, our image, or our potential on our children. So, this is the house or facet of ourselves in which we wrestle with our offspring issues.

But that just tells me that we didn't do too good a job of developing our own individuality. If we are likely to use our children as scapegoats for our own failed ego issues, it means we have not discovered how to make ourselves happy and fulfilled. We should not need to have children to get them to live it for us, should we?

The telltale sign that you have some challenging issues to work through in this respect will be heavy planets or zodiac signs residing there. As noted in the last paragraph, a common problem is the parent trying to force their own aspirations on their children, when the children have their own fifth house to honour!

Capricorn in the fifth can mean difficulty conceiving children. Well, not just children—most everything you do to get that sense of exhilaration and pride will be hard work. We might be fearful of simply playing, or deny ourselves the feeling of specialness because of embarrassment and guilt. Sometimes we might overcompensate and take on punishing amounts of hard work, which produces astonishing results. This is right for the person with a heavy fifth house because this is how they feel their personal power. Remember you can turn the lead into gold once you recognize the issue. We can't heal anything that we haven't first felt.

One more example: Scorpio in the fifth can mean words are difficult for either the child or parent to express. Nevertheless, there could be a strong bond with them—or the opposite; it is hard to reach that bond. (You'll have to work out which.) Or it could even mean that at some point you have a sexually intense, erotic lover who arouses strong feelings. What could you do to use the Scorpio fifth house effectively? How about trying burlesque dancing? The perfect way to have fun with a sexual overtone. Your fifth house will love it.

This is also the house of love affairs and romance, but not of relating in the sense of being married, or partners living together and sharing a mortgage. The fifth, sixth, and seventh houses are a metaphor for a romance that starts out in the fifth, gets adjusted into routine and service in the sixth, and then becomes the balancing act of a formal marriage with commitments in the seventh.

Romantic love makes us feel special, happy, and immortal. Our feelings about ourselves are elevated and we feel alive and inspired. This is just one type of love among others that are to be found among the symbols of astrology.

Somebody with activity in the fifth house will live out the above fairly literally. They will enjoy and partake of creative activities or drama, or will tend to have love affairs.

You might notice that your most memorable love affairs will have been with people who resemble your fifth house. For instance, if you have Pisces there, he will be a Piscean-type person. This happens particularly if you don't live out your fifth house yourself. And what happens when it ends? Then they walk away with your happiness, specialness, and confidence.

It is better to use what you have got there to develop your own importance, specialness, distinctiveness, and, eventually, happiness (all Fire attributes); then no one can walk away with it. The connection to the divine force that lives in our spirit/Fire has got to be our greatest gift and this house is one of the access points in our chart. Come here for comfort and a reason to live, love this facet of your life, and see the difference it makes.

The Ninth House

This is the final Fire house. There are none in the fourth quadrant because our importance there is negligible. However, the Fire zodiac signs can appear there and lend us some! In this facet of our lives, we search for the spiritual. It has associations with Sagittarius and Jupiter.

This house is a final act, and exploration, of belief in the divine. It is also the search for the pristine truth—the real deal and full explanation of all spiritual matters. The questing now becomes quite urgent, especially if we are getting older. And as we devour information and surge further and higher into our search, it only feeds back into greater determination.

What we are looking for has to be the purest, most flawless, immaculate, and completely incorrupt evidence of the truth that can possibly be found.

An urgent individual understanding is needed and it can't be anyone else's regurgitated, copy-and-pasted or fake thoughts.

We search for the elusive connection that feels right and we are driven to keep going. So we move forward and make another connection, and in this way we keep searching and perfecting our version of truth. The answers need to provide meaning and substance.

If we have a Masculine zodiac sign or many planets in this house, we eventually finish up teaching, which really fires our learning.

The searching and broadening of horizons also applies to foreign cultures, a source of great fascination for their difference.

The Meaning of the Feminine Earth Houses

The second, sixth, and tenth houses—or facets of our lives—are the Feminine Earth houses.

In all three of these facets of our life, we have to build something solid to sustain our bodies. When we think about it, our basic bodily needs are warmth or protection from heat, nourishment, and security from harm. Money provides choices in our ability to support and sustain ourselves and diversity for our curious natures. After that, comfort or even luxury is nice.

In the Earth houses we have a range of gifts and options to enable us to do that building. The planets and zodiac signs in them will describe the tools we have to make use of in this endeavour—or the issues that bedevil us.

At this point, it is wise to go back to the section on the Earth Element and Earth zodiac signs and read them again. The more familiar you are with the psychology of not just Earth, but all the Elements, the better your astrology will be. These Earth houses resonate with their counterparts in the zodiac belt and planets, and are so similar that I won't repeat the same material again. That makes this section shorter, but it doesn't make the houses any less important.

In fact, for individual astrological support these houses are the most important.

The Second House

This facet of our lives is associated with the first Earth sign of Taurus and the planet Venus. It is also the first of the Earth houses, and as such we'd expect it to be reasonably simple and basic, which it is. However, it also has considerable power and importance. The birth chart in which the second house sits is setting down the foundations for this person's life and, if the building isn't done properly, it could cause a problem at the wrong time—which is the case for a lot of people.

With our astrology, we can see clearly what the challenges are and take steps to remedy them. It has always been an irony that astrology can predict that a person finds it difficult to hold on to money, but then give that person "the antidote" to the loss. If they achieve financial success, then with hindsight the prediction is no longer correct.

Traditionally—and the Earth houses have good, old traditional values—this house is about substance, matter, possessions, money, income, resources, valuables, wealth/poverty, and having an appreciation of worth and value.

I'd say that's a good list and add a few more things. Warmth, security, and "body." If the first house is a metaphor for the birth of a new energetic and spiritual self, then the second house is the baby finding its fingers and toes. There is a real difference between the newborn, which is happy to be tightly swaddled, and the next stage of thumping its limbs around with gusto. Here the spirit and soul are finding out how to work the body.

In this facet of our lives, there is a natural urge to make ourselves more solid, permanent, stable, and enduring. To give ourselves more substance, which would explain why putting on weight begins here. The survival logic seems to be that the bigger we are, the more of us there is, the longer we will exist.

There is a curiosity in this house too. It is as if the baby is exploring and everything is put into the mouth for testing. Does it feel nice in the mouth? (That's the feeling of touch, taste, and smell that is also a Taurean feature.) Will it give me a nice feeling or enjoyment? People with an emphasized second house treat food with great seriousness and know a great deal about it. As with Taurus, this is to do with the senses, particularly those of taste and smell. The creaminess, sweetness, and general deliciousness of food is all so appealing and comforting.

Certainly, this house can be too indulgent, hedonistic, and acquisitive, but that is only a few expressions in a very sensitive list. In certain conditions people can starve themselves because they "hate" their body. Or they become food addicts, grow very large, and still hate their body. Or they do the healthy eating thing and attend a gym twice a day. The planets and zodiac signs in the second house will describe which way these things are likely to go.

The Sixth House

This facet of our lives is about service to all kinds of mundane, domestic, and work things. It takes care of the body's general health, plus service and duties in the domestic and work environment. That means the daily chores of washing up, cooking dinner, cleaning the house, collecting parcels from online shopping lockers, dropping the car off for a service, gardening . . . you get it. Let's just say that some of us do more sixth house work than others, even with a full-time, paid job too.

Virgo and the planet Vesta are very much associated with this house and it is because of her patronage that we can find pleasure and fulfilment when these tasks are well done. Because it is actually possible to feel good when we can look at what we have done. When the home is sparkling or we manage to tick off a whole list of chores in a day, we do feel pleased with ourselves, don't we? Well, I do anyway. This house offers the opportunity to honour our sense of duty and hard work, and in doing so we revere the Earth Element and thousands of years of offering service to the gods.

Going back to our bodies, the routines of brushing teeth, bathing, shaping eyebrows and nails along with anything else that maintains the body, all come under this facet of our lives. We also maintain our bodies by attending routine medical appointments and any other dental or beauty arrangements. Health also includes deciding on vitamin supplements, preventative or complementary medicines, and exercise routines. We may decide to take up diets or exercise to maintain our health.

And then there is our actual health and illness and the worry about such matters. Planets and zodiac signs can indicate the type of things we might suffer from. For instance, Neptune or Pisces in the sixth can indicate autoimmune diseases such as psoriasis, eczema, or allergy. In these cases, the cell walls of the skin are having difficulty maintaining themselves—Pisces is known for having a dissolving effect on bodily cells.

The Virgo resonance means that this is the house of worry too. Worry about health. Worry about missing an appointment. Worry about overindulgence. Worry that there is nothing to worry about. Guilt over obligations. Worry over guilt . . . Worried about cancer . . . Worried about money . . .

The Tenth House

This facet of our lives is naturally associated with Capricorn, but is mainly about our career. In a birth chart, the random zodiac signs and planets that land in this house will all describe the career we should best follow for maximum success, status, and achievements. However, some people don't enter into a paid career and, in that case, it can also describe how others see them and what they would have wanted to do given the chance.

It also about achievements in general. Where we aspire to achieve and create our highest achievements. It is the top of our tree. What we can look back on and feel proud of. What we want to be respected for. Our career often offers the opportunity to achieve responsibility or authority through competency and skill; a stamp of authority that this Capricorn-ruled house thoroughly approves of.

I have also noticed that it appears to represent how people view us socially—until they have a one-to-one conversation, when it moves to the first house and ascendant. The planets and zodiac signs in the tenth are seen by everyone. A public image if you like.

Now here is a strange thing. Our parents are represented by that thick black line going from the top of the chart to the bottom (see Figure 13). It is the cusp of both the tenth house and the fourth house. One of our parents demonstrated to us how to behave in the outside world, and so our tenth house describes the parent who was most dominant and influential in teaching us how we should present ourselves. When we were taught to be polite and act a certain way in public, that parent was grooming our appearance and performance. If we were told to avoid the bullies or find a grown-up to mediate and seek a diplomatic way, we might have Libra there. If we were told to go and punch the bullies back, then we might have Aries on the cusp of the house.

We might also take a vocation or career from the influence of this parent. This is often shown by a repetition of the relevant zodiac signs in both parent and child birth charts. For instance, I have an ascendant (the cusp of my first house) in late degrees of Libra. My daughter was born with her M/C (midheaven—the cusp of her tenth house in the same degree of Libra). And I was the most influential parent. Her father has his Sun in Aries and her I/C (lowest point) is in Aries. (Don't worry if you can't follow that yet!)

We become driven to follow the career suggestions in our birth chart as we get older, no matter what we trained to do or what our parents might still say. There is a nagging sense of unfulfilment if those energies haven't had their chance yet.

Let's look at some examples. If Taurus is on the midheaven, we will want to be involved with Nature, beautifying the human body, or making delicious food. We might want to build something in stone, brick, or clay that will last for ever. So building, brick-laying, carpentry, gardening, arable or dairy farming, chocolate- or sweet-making, or beauty therapy would all be good careers.

Leo is a tough one to accommodate because there are limited opportunities for performers. In which case, it might mean having a day job to pay the bills and an unpaid night job to seek the thrill of audience acclaim. And even then, it should be remembered that Leo energy is not compatible with service or being the lowest paid employee in a hierarchical setting. Self-employment of any kind works best because then Leo feels in control.

The Meaning of the Masculine Air Houses

The third, seventh, and eleventh houses—or facets of our lives—are the Masculine Air houses.

You would be wise to return to the section on the Air Element and the Air zodiac signs and reread them at this point. Because of the similarity between the zodiac signs and houses, there is little new information and no need to repeat everything here.

The Air houses provide us with three facets of our lives where we can detach from the things that came before and put another kind of order to our lives. Air is a very useful Element if we want to escape, because it offers a pair of scissors and a dotted line with the words "cut here." Each of the following Air houses offers a change of scenery and a new social environment. Fresh "air" if you like.

Air rules the logical mind. It allows us to be self-conscious, to evaluate and rationalize our lives in context. It is also the principle of communication and the exchange of ideas. It is worth repeating that Air is looking for ideas and patterns to make sense.

It is civilized and gracious to a point, seeking balance and fairness. It needs to analyze and assess using a questioning approach, because words and conversation are important to the Air Element.

Detachment is vital so that the natural circulation and synthesis between people on a social level can be monitored and understood. Because of this, it tends towards lightness and superficiality even in relationship mode. If you remember, it is opposite to Water, which clings. Air likes to separate such fusion, creating distinctions that can be studied separately.

The Third House

The house system can be thought of as a metaphor for a human life. If a baby is born in the first house and discovers how to control its body in the second house, then when it gets to the third house it is ready to separate from the mother and speak or communicate with others. Learning, as in the collection of information, is done in this house. First, we must learn a language to communicate in. Then we must practise it with siblings, or those around us in early school years.

We must learn to read and write; then we can read books and write our ideas down for others to read. It also represents the local neighbourhood because the "baby" (now a four- to six-year-old) is becoming inquisitive about the world around it. This house also represents short journeys, such as those to school; and, traditionally, our siblings can be found here.

Okay, so when we grow up, what do we use this house for then? It is still used for enquiring, learning, writing books, learning new languages, and the local neighbourhood. I'm writing a book and this endeavour is done from my third house, which has Capricorn in it. Have a guess at what that means?

The Seventh House

It is said that the seventh is about "the adjustment of enmity." I didn't know what that meant, so I looked up enmity and it said, "ill will and hostility." It is also called the house of "open enemies." Putting these clues to one side, let's go back to what I said in the opening paragraph to this section: "The Air houses . . . where we can detach from the things that came before and put another kind of order to our lives."

Putting those two opinions together still requires some clarification. What are we detaching from and what is the new kind of order? We are metaphorically cutting free of the fifth and sixth houses. We leave behind our single, autonomous individuality. In the fifth house we discovered our personal power and then in the sixth house we cleaned, served, learned domestic duties, and prepared to enter into a formal, sharing, legal commitment to another in the seventh house. So the Air of the seventh house helps us to cut free of self-sufficiency and enter the World of Two.

The seventh is mostly about the significant other. This is the "opposite" person who we seek to balance things with. If you get married in your lifetime, it is most definitely about your marriage partner. However, if you have had few relationships and no marriage, then it will represent, in descending order, a business partner, a family member, a treasured pet, and so on.

The associated planets are Venus and Juno. The associated zodiac sign is Libra.

141

Just a quick point on the opposition between the first and the seventh. "Relating to" is about recognizing differences. We "relate to" when "they" are opposite and different, not fused and the same. The World of Two is so different to the world of one, and the Element of Air is needed to get to grips with this.

The Eleventh House

In the eleventh house or facet of our lives, we seek to be part of an organized system or brotherhood; we may become "comrades" or members of a commune, but more usually it is about university or groups and associations.

With respect to the "detaching from the things that came before and put a new kind of order to our lives," this facet of our lives is about breaking free of the family and discovering like-minded people to rebel with. This house is associated with Aquarius and Uranus, so it has rebellious credentials and holds aspirations for a new paradigm. When this aspiration goes beyond a university and out into universal theory, then we get such fabulous groups as the Star Trek Fans of Northwest US Club and the Caltech Alumni Science Exchange exploring the history and impact of artificial intelligence . . . and everything in between.

This is where we can feel part of a big universal whole and part of the universal mind in the future. Hopes, wishes, dreams, visions, and ideal aspirations for humankind are in this house, far beyond the horizon . . .

The Meaning of the Feminine Water Houses

The fourth, eighth, and twelfth houses—or facets of our lives—are the Feminine Water houses.

The Water houses follow the Air houses, so the new kind of order that Air has sorted out is subject to a tsunami that sweeps everything into Water's cosmic womb once more. Remember Air resonates with height and light, while Water is pulled inwards and downwards into the fearful depths of Pluto's secret layers. In the section on the Element of Water we learned that "Water is a medium of our world and the invisible realm of dark matter and energy that flows all around us unseen and unfelt. It flows, connects, and mediates throughout Earthly and spiritual existence."

Ancient cultures realised the sap in trees and plants was connected to the same spiritual Water, which in turn the Egyptians saw as the Cosmic Ocean of the starry sky.

Spiritual Water has a mysterious "memory" that carries information about the past and its origins. I see it as the Great Soul Lake that is the repository of all memories. Others call it the "Ocean" of life, suggesting it is a deep, vast, and unknowable primordial existence.

The liquid water and spiritual Water around our planet carry communication in a different way to Air, although we haven't worked out the fine detail yet. But some declare that the vibrations of a single organism moving in water can be felt by another without any obvious communication as we know it. Multiply that by the vastness of the oceans and information gets around.

It doesn't mean that millions of independent life forms all get the same information at once; it doesn't have to go from A to Z in the same instance. (Although it might.) What if it goes from A to B, then B to C, then C to D, etc?

As I mentioned in the section on the Element of Water, our ancestors and the lives they led pass unknown feelings and experiences on to us via (what we call) the Water Element in our birth charts. For instance, the famine one of our ancestors experienced in the nineteenth century can be found latent in our epigenes. Okay, maybe that is a primordial, species-survival thing. What cannot be explained is why a woman's maternal ancestors all had babies while unmarried.

Water is very mysterious stuff. So how do you feel about having three houses full of it in your birth chart? Three portals of ancestral baggage, emotional doom, and no guidebook?

Seems like we are going to need to understand this lot really well, or drown! So here are some core facts to aid your survival. This is a bit like the life-jacket demonstration in an aircraft before a flight over water. Pay attention now, because it is too late when you are descending.

To start with, everything in your Water houses was set up, or happened, before you arrived. The karma or inheritance preceded you and was given to you by previous experiences in the ancestral line, which roll up like a snowball. Or perhaps another way of looking at it is as the passing of the family "baton" that gets handed on to the next generation in a relay race. Our grandmother handed the baton on to our mother, and our mother hands it on to us. When we say "Water has memory" we mean that a parent's DNA, epigenetic tagging, and genes all contribute to the history or memory of the family's ancestral lineage. We are learning how to read this inheritance, history, or memory by studying the zodiac signs and/or associated planets in these houses. They will tell the story. For instance, Pisces on the cusp of the fourth house could mean one of the parents was an addict or absent. (Pisces rules addiction and the yearning of loss, while in general the fourth is about a parent or parents.)

The eighth house goes further back to parents, grandparents, and great-grandparents. Aquarius on the cusp of this house suggests a family history of emotional distance and dysfunction or some sort of psychopathy. Three recent major figures of the British royal family inherited this feature and it is not hard to see why. A lack of normal family life, grandparents and parents with a high workload and national responsibilities, nanny substitutes and limited access to parents, strict boarding schools, and no one to confide in.

Now let me just stress that our Water houses are about that which comes before us, and we have to wrestle with it. By itself, Aquarius in the eighth does not suggest that this person is creating the emotional phobia; it is their inheritance. In that respect, these houses can be brutal, bringing uncivilized and tragic events into our lives, making us feel powerless and reducing life to useless, painful struggling. At the very least, "history will always repeat itself."

I am reminded of the Dementors in the Harry Potter books. At any moment I could have a Dementor chasing me through an underworld cave of Hell. Okay, there are lighter moments—the birth of a baby, sex, and the experience of love—but there are certainly as many lows as highs. Enough said: where or what is the antidote?

First of all, because the planets in these houses carry the past with them, we need to know as much as possible about our past so we can honour it and play our part in the evolution of our family line. "Interview" your oldest relatives and record their stories now. (This is a great record to pass on in any case.) Try to discover the things the "children" weren't to be told. There are websites that can help with ancestral searches. Make up the family tree with dates of birth; that is always interesting. You may be surprised which zodiac signs dominate.

Second, look at the following house, which will be a Fire house. That is what astrology says should break the energy. There lies strength and confidence. Just reach for it—you'll see.

Third, don't try to ignore the writing on the wall. Take it on without struggling against it. Pretend theses facets of your life are filled with quicksand, so struggle/denial will only dig you in deeper. Lie there and absorb.

With those tools and your new astrology skill, you are ready to process and honour those demons. I have no idea what will come up—it is different for everyone—but you will be as prepared as you can be to listen, sympathize, forgive, heal, and then lay to rest. If you do this right, those issues will not appear in the Water houses of one more family member. Job well done.

All three Water houses can carry psychic abilities.

The Fourth House

This facet of your life represents the homes you grew up in and your immediate family or the main caregivers. Those two experiences form your deep, unconscious psychological roots. Now, it is where you go to when your back is against the wall, your mental refuge. Only those who have lived with you see this other, secret side to you, and it is normally completely different to your career. This early beginning was handed to you; there was nothing you could have done to change it—it was pre-chosen. And, throughout your whole life, you will never be able to change it, for it is a finished version of you and a feeling that you will never be free from. These home-linked emotional patterns are there for good, so the conditions described by the zodiac sign and planets are from the parent (mother) before us. Our roots are anchored in this soil and we use it to grow the tree (us). This realm is inherited, it belongs to the family background, it is not our own to grow and change.

Since it is your fate and you cannot change it, you need to accept it and understand it. This house will show you how you learned to respond emotionally and what the "mothering" was like. It is where experience is being handed down through generations and is a link to our soul and its past. Perhaps there is a soul repository here. Something is being re-generated to live on through us again. We must live and experience it on behalf of the soul or matriarchal line. This may or may not be comfortable—but we are stuck with it.

The fourth is linked to the Moon and Cancer. This imagery is embedded deeply in humankind's unconscious, whether openly acknowledged or not. There are some very deep, mysterious, ancestral roots here.

The Eighth House

When we love another person, it changes us for ever—the World of Two is probably the most powerful transformation we will ever make. This facet of our lives, the eighth house, is where we share money, possessions, and penetrating emotional and sexual experiences with others. It stirs up profound and intoxicating love and passion for another, but also all the crises, vulnerabilities, and a range of feelings from jealousy to ecstasy. This house transforms us, as in the birth of a baby; this is a joyous event, but everyone would agree that it changes the quality of life completely.

Sounds good? But the trouble is we could also be activating any deeply buried rage to do with our early emotional exchange with mother. Sound unlikely? Well, you would be amazed! All kinds of brutal and unrestrained behaviour can erupt in us or around us when the eighth house opens the gates to love. This is because the unspoken family history and family curses will come right up with it. Sound scary?

Sometimes it can be, but it is even worse if we have no idea where the current emotional tsunami has come from. In the introduction to the Water houses, I suggested that you should try to discover the things "the children" weren't to be told; interview your oldest relatives and write their stories down while you still can. After 40 years or so, it will all make sense.

I suggest you do the digging into family secrets and skeletons before you find yourself in the midst of an emotional washing machine. These are the ways of the Feminine and should not be feared, for at the bottom of it they are the opportunities for personal growth our soul needs, and as we do the work, it heals the generations behind us and the generations in front of us.

And that is the main point: we are simply working on our bit of Life itself. Just one of those ants in the ant colony.

When the emotional upheaval starts, our instinct is to try to take control, but our feeble power-grabbing doesn't work best in this house. The thing to do is go along with it. Imagine yourself in quicksand and simply lie still to lessen the impact. If you try to run away, you will only take yourself with you, because you are the centre of the storm; so the journey just goes on longer.

Greek myth has the famous story of Persephone, Demeter, and Hades to illustrate how life works in these matters. The story's central message is that we cannot hold back the cycle of life and how everything must grow and transform, even when it would be lovely to keep it the same. Death and rebirth; the changing of the seasons; children growing up, getting married, and having families of their own; moving into old age and passing on. All things change.

The zodiac sign on the cusp of the eighth is important. We will draw people to us who resonate with that sign, and they will act like catalysts in our lives, taking us into the phantom's lair or deep primordial feelings and experiences.

The other perspective that should be flagged up is that of love. This is the place where the euphoric, delightful, intoxicating feelings of love are at their most intense.

Often, people with this house emphasis work with people in crisis situations—drugs workers, counsellors, doctors, bereavement workers, paramedics, hospice staff, etc—and for them, the crisis environment feels like home. They rise to every demand without fear or revulsion and feel totally fulfilled by the experience.

On a practical level, legacies and inheritances can appear when the eighth is activated.

In the introduction to the Water houses, I mention that an antidote to each of them is the Fire house that comes after it, and I want to remind you of that. The ninth house with its wonderful sense of freedom and confidence is just what the cosmos ordered.

The Twelfth House

When the Sun rises above the horizon it is rising into the twelfth house. And what I am about to say may surprise you. That part of the sky seems to weaken or dissolve the Earthly psychological strength of anything in it, even the Sun. It may be because the Earth's atmosphere is distorting the usual rays, light rays, and waves. However, it is what it is. The puzzle of the twelfth's weakness will never be solved in this book; I will leave that one to future multiverse astrologers! In the meantime, what does seem to be stronger is the connection to the source or the other side. I think it is fair to say that this facet of our lives is a portal to a dimension beyond ours, which weakens the strength of any planets or zodiac signs in order to get a look-in.

People with an emphasized twelfth house serve a public or larger cause. Some may well be able to tap into collective feelings and big sea-changes in public opinion. Others hear messages from another world and act as a vehicle. Sometimes it denotes a lifetime of public service or a monastic lifestyle. They have to acknowledge something sacred or spiritual. Astrology books will tell you it is the house of hospitals and prisons (and package holidays, for that matter) because you have no will or independence. You are told when to eat, sleep, and wake.

It attracts those who are ready to give everything up for spiritual causes, religions, or a lifetime's service to stray cats. The need to ignore their own wants and just give their lives to such a cause comes from a redemptive urge that can be found in Pisces, the ruling planet Neptune, and the twelfth house. It has something to do with taking on all that has been so wrong in the world and wanting to put it right. They have just got to heal and fix everything to make up for it. When they give up their will to this force, they feel so much better.

Unfortunately, addictive substances can become the force that overwhelms their will and, honestly, if this house is packed with personal planets, there is not much hope of them giving up the addiction either; it just feels so right.

If, for some reason, the person is able to create and maintain a strong sense of self-discipline and not get lost in the metaphysical side, they will be able to add something to the long-term history of their ancestral line or the collective. They are also needed to live something out for the "whole of life." Their lives are involved with a "bigger" plan.

There is still something ancestral and past-life about this house, as there is with the other Water houses, but quite often it goes back so many generations the information seems to blur into wanting to make amends for "something" and that is about it.

I think there is a hidden cosmic truth in this house and I want to point out that if there is, then this is where you come the closest to learning about it, because this is your own personal connection to the cosmos. All your houses are very, very individual to you. No one else has exactly the same configuration as you, because the house size and the position of the signs over them changes in a matter of seconds. It is also dependent on the exact spot you were born in. Even twins have slightly different birth charts.

We will cover more of the importance of your houses later, but for now let's get back to the exciting bit about the twelfth house. As I was saying, this is your own individual portal to the cosmos, and most especially to Nut, the Egyptian Great Sky Goddess and mother to all. She was the water of the sky and space. Some of her names were Goddess of Life, Mistress of All, and She who Bore the Gods. She swallowed the Sun at night and gave birth to it in the morning.

As far as I know, the Ancient Egyptians were the only ones to recognize the infinity of the sky as Feminine and the Earth as Masculine. The cosmos was female, watery, and mother to all, in which case, this is how you can reach her: through your twelfth. My reasoning is that the Water houses are our own personal contact with the past and our origins. The fourth and the eighth are more the family line and its ancestors. The twelfth is a Water house and infinite in nature.

I'm going to pick up on the theme of making amends for something; on the need to redeem ourselves when it comes to the Water energy in this house.

Somewhere in another dimension there is a Great Soul Lake, which holds all the memories of everyone who has lived and died. This is

Feminine in nature and it is quite possible that a way can be found to access it psychically. If so, that person could be in touch with all that is sad and mourned, all the kisses that went un-kissed, all the love not given, all the feelings not offered . . . According to Water, all these are transgressions that will be mourned and not forgiven, as everything sinks into oblivion once more.

Okay, maybe that is a bit morbid, but we are talking Water here. To get the messages from your twelfth, you need to meditate with the zodiac sign on the cusp at the top of your thought. That is your route in. Good luck.

The Twelve Houses Divided into Groups

Let's do a quick recap on the houses: Just as the zodiac signs can be divided into groups of two, three, and four, so can the houses. There are many similarities between the houses and zodiac signs. For instance, Taurus is resonant with the second house and they share many of the same descriptive words.

Three Houses in a Group—Same Element

- The Fire houses (first, fifth, and ninth) look to the future and offer facets of strength and potential confidence. They help our quest to exist and be powerful.

- The Earth houses (second, sixth, and tenth) then give our dreams form, take care of our bodily needs, and manifest our striving for individuation.

- Each of the Air houses (third, seventh, and eleventh) offers a change of scenery and a new social environment. We can detach from the things that came before and put another kind of order to our lives.

- The Water houses (fourth, eighth, and twelfth) represent love in three different ways. The unconditional love of mother. The conditional love for a partner. The mysterious universal, or cosmic love. They also carry the karma and unresolved issues of the ancestors and the past for us to heal and transform.

Four Houses in a Group—Same Modality

- The first, fourth, seventh, and tenth are all cardinal houses and they try to lead and instigate.
- The second, fifth, eighth, and eleventh are all fixed houses and they try to preserve and sustain, keeping things the same.
- The third, sixth, ninth, and twelfth houses are all mutable and they easily accept change and adjustment.

Two Houses in a Group—Same Polarity

- The first and seventh are Masculine and they are about one becoming two.
- The second and eighth are Feminine and they are about resources and sharing.
- The third and ninth are Masculine and about learning and higher wisdom.
- The fourth and tenth are Feminine and about growing up and moving out into the world.
- The fifth and eleventh are Masculine and about appreciation of self and then the group.
- The sixth and twelfth are Feminine and about service to self and serving others.

There are some general points to be made about the houses as your own personal and individual take on life.

It is most probable that there is no one else on Earth with the same birth chart as you. Another baby would have to be born right next to you and breathe its first breath at exactly the same time. If they were born a mile or two away, they will not have the same birth chart as you; in fact there could be some quite significant differences. If they were born a few minutes either side of your first breath, they will not have the same birth chart; and, again, there could be some quite important differences.

You really, really are unique. And it is the houses that make this so, for the structure of them moves very quickly during the day, and each day is a little bit different. And yet so few astrologers even appreciate that point. To fully understand a birth chart, you have to know your houses and how the zodiac signs affect that facet of your life.

This is where so much behavioural understanding comes from.

The eight planets only enhance or add to that information and I believe learning about them should only come when you can competently read a chart without them.

Let's try this out.

A Small Sample Reading for Taurus on the Cusp of the Eighth House

Your friend/client is having difficulties with a romantic relationship. She is besotted with him, but although he seemed so keen to start with, now he is leaving longer gaps between meeting up. They had a very active sexual life initially, but now he seems willing to let that go too. She is desperate and wishes she knew where she is going wrong.

You understand from reading all about the eighth house that this might be a house or facet of her life worth looking at. What information can you glean? We will use the birth chart in figure 12, but we will need to keep an eye on Figure 13 too, because it has key words that can help us understand the psychology of the houses. For instance, the psychology of the eighth house is "Feminine, Fixed, Water." Just by reading those three words, what do we know?

The Feminine polarity tells us that this is a hidden facet of our lives with buried meaning. Natural caution will be evident. Unconscious planning and waiting can be invoked.

The Fixed overlay tells us there is nothing new here; the tradition, rituals, and magic will transform in the way they always have. Birth or death, the cycle of life will prevail.

The Water Element speaks of karma, family history, destiny, and hidden passions.

The eighth house is where we share money, possessions, and penetrating emotional experiences with significant others. It stirs up profound and intense passions, plus a range of emotions from jealousy to ecstasy. All activity is pivoted on ancestral history and past experiences. Control seems essential but our feeble power-grabs are useless and usually make things worse. The antidote? Imagine yourself in quicksand and simply lie still to lessen the pain.

But that lot is all packed into everyone's eighth house. What makes it different is the sign on the cusp, which in this case is Taurus. Now, you can read further into this facet of your client's life.

The sign on the cusp leads the person into the primordial water of the eighth house.

Now there's a problem! I can hear the bull stamping from here! This is an uncomfortable place for Taurean energy if things aren't going to plan. The Taurean need to hold and control just gets worse when painful emotions start welling up. Taurus does not know what to do with these terrifying, primordial emotions. What it wants is the security of stability—and now. Then the vicious cycle begins; she gets more upset and starts making demands . . . he doesn't think the demands are reasonable (whether they are or not) and gets more distant . . . She gets more upset and makes more demands . . . He is fed up with all the demands . . . You can see where this is going.

Your friend/client would be well advised to be cleverer with her Taurean skills of sensuality and allure, and hide the overt control elements. My advice is to keep thinking about the quicksand and simply lie still to lessen the drowning effect; to turn the control element of Taurus to her own advantage, by controlling herself.

Then on the occasions that she does see him, she should make sure that the divine diva boudoir is in full-on Taurus mode—the soft skin, the lingerie, the perfume, music, etc. Your client/friend's eighth house is in the Water Element, Feminine in polarity, and fixed in nature. Taurus was made for this. What better facet of herself to engage in a delightfully Taurean, persuasive way?

Advise her not to answer the phone a few times after that, using that strong Taurus control, and that should sort things out.

This is quite a lot to learn, but once again, when you have learned it it helps enormously with the psychology.

The Importance of the Cross

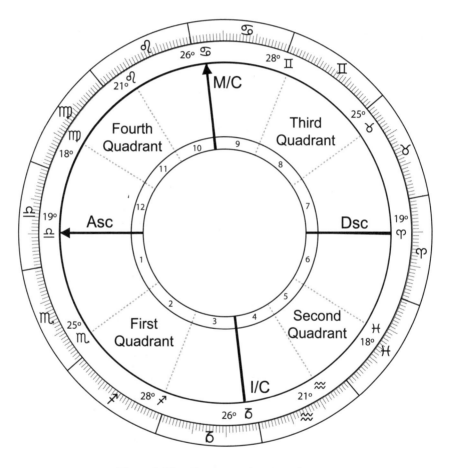

Fig. 14: The Cross, Angles, Quadrants

As you look at Figure 14 you will see the cross shape. The lines are thicker and there is an arrowhead at the top of the vertical one and on the left of the horizontal one.

You are looking at a representation of the Earth and sky around you at the moment of your birth.

The thick horizontal line is the horizon to the east and west of you. The **ascendant** (Asc.) is the left-hand point of the thick horizontal line and the **descendant** (Dsc.) is the right point of the same line.

The thick vertical line goes into the centre of the Earth at the bottom and up into the midheaven in the sky at the top. The **midheaven** (MC) is the top point of the vertical line and the lowest point (**imum coeli**—IC) is at the bottom.

They are roughly in a cross shape and the four points are called the **angles**.

The cross shape divides the circle into four quarters or **quadrants**. The quadrants have three houses each. So, there are twelve houses in total, the same number as zodiac signs.

The houses numbered one to six in a birth chart are the ones below the horizon at the moment of a person's birth. Some of these can be quite deep and difficult to get to know. They were on the other side of the Earth at the moment of birth, so the "rays" had to get through the dense Earth to reach the newborn baby.

The houses numbered six to twelve have a different feel to the majority of the first six; they are more open and public. These were in the sky above at the moment of birth, so the "rays" reached the baby easily.

Now let's go back to the thick, cross shape in the birth chart, and the four angles. The left-hand one, the Asc., is most important. The top one, the MC, is next most important. After that, the Dsc. and IC are about equal. The houses after the angles are called angular or cardinal houses, and they are important houses.

The Angles

I have never been able to get out of my mind the metaphorical image of a human strapped to a wheel at the moment of birth and how the birth chart symbolizes that. (And now you won't be able to get it out of your mind either!) So, picture yourself in the middle of that birth chart. Maybe you are sitting in the little circle at the centre. Around you is the structure of the houses, which are actually dependent on that cross shape, which we call the angles. That cross, with all its information, is so important; it is as if we are hanging on it for our whole life.

Going back to the houses: in those twelve facets of your life, there is information about your past, present, and future. Your strengths, weaknesses, opportunities, and threats. It's like a blueprint for your life, and all you have to do . . . is read it. (Sounds easy, doesn't it?)

The Ascendant

First of all, the ascendant (Asc.) is also the cusp of the first house, and arguably the most immediately important part of the birth chart. This is because when we first meet someone, this is the bit we meet. You could call it the "outside" of you. If you can imagine yourself as a house, then this is the front door. I like to think of it as the neck of a wine bottle, with the rest of your birth chart in the bottle. Whatever bit of you is about to be used, it has to come through the neck of that bottle and gets "coloured" or altered by it.

I was taught that the Asc. is "the way in which you do things." It is there from birth—as is everything, but there are some things in the chart we grow into over the years, and others that never change; they are used from the beginning. The Asc. is one such chart point.

Perhaps it is useful to see it as a cloak that covers everything. It's also like a mask that we look through. In one-to-one personal encounters, other people see our Asc. first. Or, putting that another way, personal first encounters are led by the Asc. The Sun will show through as we get to know someone better. If one of the two people meeting is in a professional position, however, such as a parent meeting a teacher, or a patient meeting a doctor, then the patient or parent would be seeing the MC or midheaven of the doctor or teacher.

The Asc. describes how we greet the world and approach life. It describes the moment we came into life. It could describe what the birth was like. Capricorn on the Asc. might be describing a long hard labour. Aries on the Asc. might suggest a quick and aggressive appearance, because an Aries Asc. will leap forward into life and want everything to be speedy.

The natal horoscope is drawn for the exact moment of the first breath because it is only then that the newborn human begins to exchange energy with the universe as a *separate* individual, no longer using the mother's body. At the moment of the first breath, the infant begins its own life within our dimension. The birth chart, with its combination of a spinning zodiac belt and a separate and differently spinning house system, is like a photograph taken at exactly the right moment. A brief snapshot in time, and it forever records the influential electromagnetic environment at that exact moment. That is your birth chart.

The Midheaven, *Medium Coeli*, or MC

This is the angle at the top of the birth chart (see Figure 12 if you are getting confused here). And I guess that position tells us a lot about what it represents. It is where the world can see us. We are on show, so the zodiac sign there is going to be important. If we are on show . . . what are we showing?

Well, let's say we have a Fire sign at that point; then we will be fairly obvious and noticeable. If it is an Earth sign, we will be slow, steady, and competent. An Air sign on the MC will appear to be socially gracious and communicative. Water signs up there want to be hidden; the limelight makes them feel nervous.

Usually, the midheaven describes the career or vocation, and if it doesn't the client will have difficulties in this area. Some zodiac signs, like Scorpio, lend themselves to an array of different career paths, and, so long as they are "masterful" at it, all will be well. But there are some signs with quite a narrow bandwidth when it comes to career, and if they are in the wrong one there will be a history of discord and unfulfillment.

A Leo midheaven, for instance, can have a lot of difficulty finding the right opportunity. There aren't that many openings for out-of-work actors in London's West End! In which case they can finish up waiting tables, and oh my, that often goes very wrong. In my view, it is more important to meet the needs of the zodiac sign than anything else. Therefore two careers is a possibility, one to pay the bills and one to keep the midheaven happy. So, our Leo midheaven could be self-employed as a plumber, *and* be a lead member of an amateur dramatics group.

The Leo MC is only concerned with how the world sees it, and the applause of the audience is everything. Money is unimportant to Leo; therefore appearing in an unpaid drama group is a great option. The additional, self-employment option is mainly for money, but at least then this person is their own boss, and that is important for the Leo MC too.

The Descendant

This chart point is also the cusp of your seventh house and where "the World of Two" is described. "The significant other" is a much-used phrase to define it. More often than not, it describes the marriage partner.

If you have Taurus on the Dsc. then the likelihood is that your most important relationship, or relationships, will be with someone who has an important birth chart point that lands near your Dsc. or in your seventh house.

The Lowest Point, *Imum Coeli*, or IC

Our final angle is the lowest point, *imum coeli* or IC. Most astrologers refer to it as the IC. This point is the cusp of the fourth house and it is in Water. So what is this about? It's about the family, roots, the past, the early home environment.

For predictive purposes, it also represents the current home, just as the opposite end, the MC, also represents the current job.

The zodiac sign on the IC describes one of the parents (sometimes both) and the early home environment. Here is a question for you: if Aries is on the IC, what was the early home life like? Angry? Significant arguments and fights? Lots of sport? Vibrant? Correct!

Reading the Ascendant and Midheaven Together

Let's say we have a client with the midheaven in Leo and the ascendant in Scorpio. How is this going to work out?

Well, the first thing I'm going to say is that you have to take it back to basics, as I said somewhere near the beginning of this book.

Start with the polarities. One is Masculine and one is Feminine and, as we know, these will pull in opposite directions. One (which one?) will pull inwards and want to hide, the other will push outwards and want to be on show.

Clients with this sort of clash can spend a lifetime perfecting schizophrenia (joking) or they can perfect the art of splitting themselves between the two—first giving the Leo its 15 minutes of fame (daily!) and then withdrawing for the brooding and preferred silence of Scorpio. The trick is to see yourself in a carriage with your Scorpio horse and Leo horse pulling in conflicting directions. Now talk to them. Reassure Leo that it can have its time on the stage with an audience, if it will just put up with Scorpio's impenetrable, dark, and secretive ways at a different time. One horse gets its way, then the other one does.

It is perfectly possible to allow or encourage yourself to go through life in this way. In fact, it is probably the only way. Otherwise, the two steps forward and two steps back—or, the internal jealous anguish at watching others have the audience you so desperately crave—will drive you nowhere.

One thing you do want to be noting is the fixed modality. Both of these signs are of a fixed nature and therefore extremely stubborn and intransigent. You might want to chat to the client about learning to be more flexible.

If the midheaven and ascendant are working together, we see a relaxed and fluid expression that can lend itself to great communication of ideas and purpose. An Air and Fire combination must be nice to "operate," while Fire and Fire can be hard to control but useful if you can get to the point of being a great leader without treading on toes!

When I have spoken to clients with both midheaven and ascendant in Water, I have always swooned at their gentleness; but of course they really struggle with bullying behaviour. They make the most amazing psychics and healers though.

Water and Air combinations work well because the Water modifies Air's harsh logic and emotional disdain. On the other hand, the gentle Water side is probably grateful for the Masculine backup!

There really are too many combinations to comment on here, but do some of your own research, because it is fascinating.

Quadrants

The first quadrant has no Water house; we talked about this in the Cancer section. Although we receive love from the beginning, we are not able to do anything with it until we have developed and organized our knowledge banks, memory, and schemas—our Gemini Air skills. It is after this that we can recognize and organize sensitive experiences, emotions, and feelings. Before then, we are in an instinctive, developing state with simple, primitive reflexes only.

The second quadrant has no Air house because we are concentrating on ourselves only and have no need of relationship principles. We can already talk and collect information, but we need to develop a protective ego before we start to power-share.

The third quadrant has no Earth house, but then the sixth house gave us ample opportunity to clean and feather the nest and get our health and garden in peak condition before we start to concentrate on less earthy, practical matters. In this quadrant we are learning to relate "to" things.

There is no Fire house in the fourth quadrant. The need to be "special" and individual does not naturally sit in this part of the chart. Only the collective matters here.

Interception

As you now know, there are twelve zodiac signs, each taking up 30 degrees of a circle. These drape over the houses, which can be more than 30 degrees wide, so a sign can be trapped inside a house. The sign doesn't sit on the cusp (beginning) of a house. This is important.

The cusps of the houses are active places for predictive techniques and are also associated with planetary movements. However, more importantly, they give a zodiac sign a place to express from. That is how the person experiences and uses the gifts of the zodiac sign. Without that platform or outlet, the zodiac sign is locked away and difficult to access, so it frustrates the person.

When you see an intercepted sign, remember there will be issues around it. Let's say it is Leo that is intercepted; straight away, you know that person has difficulty feeling confident, or believing themselves to be special. They may suffer from low self-esteem.

Let's look at another example. If it were Taurus that is intercepted, what does that signify for this person?

It might be easier to think what Taurus does represent, then work out the reverse of those qualities. So, instead of a person with a careful or cautious approach to money, you might find that they overplay this quality and behave like a miser, living in austere conditions. Perhaps they overplay their sensuality in a lewd or unrestrained way. Or deny any attraction to plants and nature, preferring instead to let gifted house plants die.

So, to repeat, when the sign does not cover a house cusp, it may not express itself in the usual way. It inverts or becomes distorted.

That concludes the most important basics in the practice of reading astrology from a birth chart. However, you may already be aware that there are so many other astrological techniques. For instance, we can use differently constructed charts to inform us about the quality of a relationship and the pitfalls to avoid, or the successes to develop and concentrate on. We can forecast or predict all manner of things from the weather to national issues or personal milestones. Transiting astrology will give us the daily mood of the electromagnetic environment of the solar system and the atmosphere around us . . . Horary astrology will give us the answer to a question . . . There is nothing astrology cannot do.

For now, however, you are concentrating on learning and practicing the art of understanding the behaviour of individuals by reading the results of the zodiac signs around the angles and houses of a natal or birth chart.

Let's Do Some Astrology! A Sample Reading

Believe it or not, you are now able to "read" astrology. Furthermore, good-quality astrology with a revealing psychological basis to it, and the potential to help people understand themselves better.

Look again at Figure 12. This is a real birth chart with the planets removed, because you don't need planets yet. You can do perfectly good astrology without them, and even when you do eventually include them, you will always be a better astrologer for learning it this way. When students include planets from the beginning, they never go back and do the groundwork with the houses as thoroughly as we have done. This makes a massive difference between being a skim-the-surface, pop astrologer and one who understands the outer and inner cosmos in a really in-depth way.

We will start with the ascendant sign and the midheaven sign. How are they getting along? The Asc. is in Libra and MC in Cancer, both cardinal signs, which means this person likes to initiate and lead. Both Libra and Cancer have a say in relationships, so perhaps this person is a relationship or family counsellor?

Before we go on, there is a special rule for Capricorn in the houses. Normally the sign on the house cusp is the one we should pay primary attention to in our reading, because, no matter what comes later in a house, the sign on the cusp is always stronger. However, this rule is broken when Capricorn is involved; even if Capricorn starts more than halfway through a house, it is still influential.

We are going to find Capricorn next, because, as we know, that sign causes hardship, so the client struggles with that facet of their life. These issues will stick out, because we don't forget our pain.

In the chart we are reading, Capricorn is on the cusp of the fourth house, but starts in the third house. So our reading begins with the astrologer (you) asking: "It looks like there were some challenges in your education, something held you back, can you remember what that might be?" (Go back and read Capricorn and third house if you need to.) Capricorn brings challenges and the third house is early education. In the conversation that follows, it is revealed that the client had to change schools very rapidly throughout the early years. She explains that she never learned the names of the other pupils before she was moved on again. Because you know that Capricorn delays ability, and because the client admits schooling was challenging, you could now mention this. The client might then contribute that she did think she had mild dyslexia that was completely missed, so she really struggled to learn. She has since identified that she is also a slow learner who really needed extra support from home, but her young and poorly educated mother was unable to help. She was told she was being lazy and not concentrating. She always felt ashamed of her performance.

After validating and explaining the very real barriers to learning in the client's chart, which she probably didn't understand and had never really examined before, the client says she feels so much better.

And there may be other things to do with the same astrological evidence. So the astrologer could ask: "It seems there might also have been difficulties with siblings?" Why is the astrologer asking that? Because siblings are a third-house subject.

The client replies that only recently she realised her sister was on the autistic spectrum, but again, too many schools and a very young mother with limited life experience, so nothing was diagnosed. The client couldn't understand why her sister was so difficult and why they couldn't seem to have a meaningful relationship. Again, validation is so helpful.

Capricorn also covers the cusp of the fourth house, meaning challenges in the home, roots, past, and family too.

So you ask, "Do you mind if we talk about your childhood home life?" Depending on the client's capacity to unpack this, it could take another twenty minutes of supportive astrological confirmation from you, the astrologer.

We still haven't finished those two houses yet. Sagittarius is on the cusp of the third house and wants including. (Normally, I'd cover the cusp zodiac sign first, but not when Capricorn is involved—pain comes first.) Now remember, this is a Masculine Air house where communication comes easy. Sagittarius is an exuberant Masculine Fire sign and so this will facilitate and excite the outpouring of words. Hence, the client just babbles on, without holding back. So she might find that she regularly says the wrong thing, treads on toes, and gets herself into trouble.

As the astrologer, you could now explain this phenomenon to the client. "Because exuberant energy is being used when you chat, you must often say more than you meant to."

"Oh yes," says the client, "I could bite my tongue off sometimes. I seem to open my mouth to change feet—but less so as I get older."

The improvement with age is natural, both Sagittarius and Capricorn mellow with age. When we are younger, the fear of Capricorn and the arrogance of Sagittarius made the talking and learning of the mutable third house a harrowing place.

The third house covers the transport you use to move around locally. Car, bus, bicycle, electric scooter? How about the choice of car? How does Sagittarius affect that? How often is the car replaced? In this case it turns out that the client drives a fast, bright red sports car. Well yes, Fire . . . it makes sense. Yet, there is more. Sagittarius aspires to the best and so does Capricorn. So, the sports car is a quality brand with a long life expectancy.

Out of interest, how does that fit with the tenth house with its theme of "How the world sees us?" Well, there we find Leo energy, the middle Fire sign; and, if you remember, Leo really cares about how the audience views things. Leo loves the colour red. And that red sports car is just the ticket. Hence the client has only ever owned four cars in her life: two white sports cars and two red ones! She tends to keep them for many, many years, which may be a Capricorn thing.

I'll just pause for a moment. Are you amazed at the amount of information that is available to you, the student astrologer, using just zodiac signs and houses? As I keep saying, you don't need planets to read the story of a person's life; what we have already learned in this book is deep and revealing.

Because we have already moved to the tenth house, I suggest you carry on from here for a while. Cancer is on the cusp/midheaven, so you should expect the career to be in something nurturing or family oriented. And yes, the client worked in the family business from time to time. She eventually settled as a chef—and, actually, feeding people comes naturally to Cancer.

But look! The rest of that house and by far the greater portion of it is in Leo, but it is intercepted. (Go back and read the Interception section if you don't remember.) Surely Leos don't serve? And they don't. There were clashes and power struggles for much of the time, until the client became self-employed, then it worked better. She became a celebrity chef by winning a national award for her cooking, but still liked to remain in the kitchen, out of the public eye.

Why wasn't she pushing to get the audience that Fire craves? Why did she hang back from the limelight?

Because Leo is intercepted in the tenth, and Cancer on the MC actually makes her quite shy.

But there is more . . . Have a look at the fifth house. Go back to the section on this house and read it again. (Repetition is how you learn astrology.)

The fifth house is where we will find our power, and the zodiac sign is the energy we are given to achieve this. Now, have a think about that. How will Pisces energy help the client boost her sense of confidence to the point that she takes the stage and basks in the limelight? Well, it won't, will it? Pisces dissolves egos, it doesn't enhance them.

The client's Fire spirit is being muffled by Water wherever we look at it. This will be creating internal and external stress. She will be attracting power struggles and sometimes lack of achievement as the Fire fails to accomplish what it is driven to do.

This was all reaching nerve-wracking status when, in her late thirties, she fell pregnant and gave birth to a disabled child. In just a year, the course of her whole life changed for ever as the baby needed a lot of care, so she gave up her full-time catering career for good. The Water on the cusp of the tenth and fifth houses won in the end. Fire just hadn't been able to fully do its thing. Now the client was a carer, first and foremost (Water Element), with a part-time job in admin work.

I'm going to stop there because I think you have seen enough to get how it all works. Now, finally the moment you have been waiting for . . . you can start to read your own birth chart!

Now You Can Read Your Own Birth Chart

Thankfully computers have taken all the hard work out of constructing a map of the heavens at the moment of your birth, so you don't need to. That will save many hours of angst, I can tell you.

You will need an accurate time of birth to use this system. If you are in the USA, this is easy; it is on your birth certificate. If you are in the UK it isn't, but your mother has the time written in the birth notes held in her medical history. She has to apply for this information, but it is her legal right to be given it.

Get as much information from relatives as you can about family birth times and save it for the future. One day you will be glad you did. Go into lofts and find old baby books and the baby's hospital wristband if you can. Everyone keeps them, so where did they go? There are a few questions that usually jog memories—ask about daylight, mealtimes, home or hospital birth.

If you still haven't got a time of birth, it is a challenge, but there are still some options. Find out what the client's career involves and put the appropriate zodiac sign on the cusp of the 10th house. So for example, if they are in telephone sales, go for Gemini. Sports coach? Go for Aries. Then check out where this leaves the Asc. If it's in Virgo, ask them if they worry a lot. If it's in Cancer, are they shy and reticent? (If you know your zodiac signs, those questions will make sense.) You are asking questions that will confirm the zodiac sign on the Asc. and M/C. If the answers resonate and those two points check out, trust that chart. This simple rectification has always worked for me.

Psychological astrology is very much about understanding your pain and getting to know why the same things happen again and again. When you have that knowledge, you can make better choices for yourself. The greatest gift of the techniques you have just learned is *not* needing to ask, "When is my boyfriend coming back?" Instead, you can find out why he left. And you will also know what to watch out for in the future.

Now you need to get loads of practice in what you have learned so far.

The astrology technique you have learned would have gone down well with the Ancient Egyptians because, for them, the planets had no meaning and they weren't even deities. The inclusion of planets in astrology came from the Babylonians, Greeks, and India.

Now it is time to get a copy of your birth chart in front of you. Check out every single house and reread the zodiac signs that fall there. You are learning about yourself in a way that wasn't possible before. Allow yourself "therapy time" with this information. There will be revelations that justify something you have always known but couldn't put your finger on. There will be sadness, and when there is, give yourself the red love and find a cuddly bear to love. (Or contact me for a session?)

Most of all? Make sure you dwell on how great you are too!

You can print out your birth chart
according to the teachings in this book
from the astro.com website:

www.astro.com/horoscopes

Further instructions on this can be found at:

www.alisonchesterlambert.com

Construct a Birth Chart
with Astro.com

You can use **www.astro.com** to construct a birth chart in the style described in this book.

It is important to register and sign in FIRST, or the following will not be available.

To create a chart:

- Click on (**Free**) **Horoscopes** in the main navigation
- Go to the section **Horoscope Drawings & Data**
- Then click on **Extended Chart Selection**
- Now you select your options:
- ~ Under **Birth data**, select a chart to work with
- ~ Under **Sections**, *'Round'* is default; leave this choice as it is
- ~ From **Chart type** select: *Natal Chart Wheel*
- ~ Select **Chart drawing style**: *Anglo with Zodiac*
- ~ Under **Zodiac and Houses**, pick **House System**: *Campanus* (NOT default)
- ~ And from **Zodiac**, select *Tropical* and *Geocentric* (default selections)
- ~ Under **Display and calculation options >> Miscellaneous**, select: *draw no planets*
- Finally click on the green button entitled: **Show the chart**

The Astrology Reading Cards

This book is a natural extension of the very popular *Astrology Reading Cards* set. The cards illustrate the key ideas behind psychological astrology and this book supports your learning of the theory.

Self-help astrological advice has never been easier to attain than with this spirit-guiding card deck. Featuring three sets of cards—the Zodiac Signs, the Planets, and the Houses—advice seekers can select a card from each set and then use the book of guidelines to interpret the answer. There are cards for each of the zodiac signs with the characteristics of each sign, cards for the planets and their characteristics or symbolism, and cards for each of the houses in astrology with images on them that they represent.

Featuring stunning artwork from a master artist, these cards take all the complexity out of astrological readings, and places the power firmly into the hands of the reader who hopes to gain insight into their future.

ISBN 9-781-84409-581-0

Bibliography

Aïvanhov, Omraam Mikhaël. *The Mysteries of Fire and Water*. Cedex, France: Prosveta, 1993.

Aïvanhov, Omraam Mikhaël. *The Zodiac, Key to Man and to the Universe*. Cedex, France: Prosveta, 1999.

Arroyo, Stephen. *Astrology, Psychology, and the Four Elements*. Nevada: CRCS Publications, 1975.

Arroyo, Stephen. *Relationships and Life Cycles*. California: CRCS Publications, 1993.

Daniélou, Alain. *The Myths of Gods and India*. Rochester, Vermont: Inner Traditions, 1991.

Filbey, John, and Peter Filbey. *Astronomy for Astrologers*. Wellingborough, Northamptonshire: Aquarian Press, 1984.

Goodman, Linda. *Linda Goodman's Love Signs*. London: Pan Books, 1980.

Goodman, Linda. *Linda Goodman's Sun Signs*. New York: Taplinger Publishing, 1971.

Greene, Liz. *Astrology for Lovers*. London: Thorsons, 1999.

Greene, Liz. *"The Art of Scuba Diving: Understanding the Water Houses"*. Lecture, Regent's College, London. 10 March 2002.

Greene, Liz. *The Astrology of Fate*. York, Maine: Samuel Weiser, 1984.

Greene, Liz. *"The Fire Houses"*. Lecture, Regent's College, London. 30 June 2002.

Greene, Liz. *The Outer Planets and Their Cycles*. California: CRCS Publications, 1983.

Greene, Liz, and **Howard Sasportas**. *Dynamics of the Unconsci s*. London: Arkana, The Penguin Group, 1988.

Greene, Liz, and **Howard Sasportas**. *The Inner Planets*. York, Maii : Samuel Weiser, 1993.

Idemon, Richard. *The Magic Thread, Astrological Chart Interpretation Using Depth Psychology*. York, Maine: Samuel Weiser, Inc. 1996.

Idemon, Richard. *Through the Looking Glass, a Search for Self in the Mirror of Relationships. Vol 5*, "Seminars in Psychological Astrology". York, Maine: Samuel Weiser, Inc. 1992.

Louis, Anthony. *Horary Astrology Plain and Simple*. Woodbury, Minnesota: Llewellyn Publications, 2002.

Rudhyar, Dane. *Astrological Signs, the Pulse of Life*. Boulder & London: Shambhala, undated work.

Sasportas, Howard. *The Twelve Houses*. London: Thorsons, 1998.

Tompkins, Sue. *Aspects in Astrology*. Dorset, UK: Element Books, 1989.

Walker, Robert G., and **Howard Sasportas**. *The Sun Sign Career Guide*. London: Arrow Books. 1989.

Wattles, Wallace. *The Science of Getting Rich*. Holyoke: Elizabeth Towne Co., 1910.

Index

Index

About the Author

Alison Chester-Lambert, MA, is a psychological astrologer and author of five publications including *Astrology Reading Cards* and *Greek Mythology Reading Cards*. She was also the in-house astrologer for BBC 2's *Daily Politics* show and has American TV and BBC 5 Live credits. Over the years she has worked as a horoscope writer for all the popular UK astrology journals and had a long-running regular column in the *Astrological Journal*. More recently Alison has been a regular contributor to *Mail Online*.

After achieving a Masters degree in the study of cultural astronomy and astrology, Alison had research papers published in the academic, peer-reviewed *Correlation* journal, and **astro.com** has recently republished some of her seminal work.

Now one of the most consulted astrologers worldwide, with a client list of thousands, Alison is best known for her ability to break down the complexities of astrology into easy-to-understand segments, revealing how to quickly decode a person's strengths, weaknesses, challenges, and opportunities with psychological astrology.

For more information see:
www.alisonchesterlambert.com

FINDHORN PRESS

Life-Changing Books

Learn more about us and our books at
www.findhornpress.com

For information on the Findhorn Foundation:
www.findhorn.org